The Histories of the Latin American Church

D1264037

The Histories of the Latin American Church

A Brief Introduction

Joel Morales Cruz

Fortress Press
Minneapolis

9/9/15
$ LN 24.50

THE HISTORIES OF THE LATIN AMERICAN CHURCH

A Brief Introduction

Copyright © 2014 Fortress Press. All rights reserved. Except for brief quotations in critical articles or reviews, no part of this book may be reproduced in any manner without prior written permission from the publisher. Visit http://www.augsburgfortress.org/copyrights/ or write to Permissions, Augsburg Fortress, Box 1209, Minneapolis, MN 55440.

Cover image: © Thinkstock; BlueWallTexture/123381129/miceneo/iStock/Thinkstock; MarbleBackground/478870317/rakratchada/iStock/Thinkstock; MexicanCemetary/478334641/Evgeny_Kozhevnikov/iStock/Thinkstock

Cover design: Alisha Lofgren

Library of Congress Cataloging-in-Publication Data

Print ISBN: 978-1-4514-8894-4

eBook ISBN: 978-1-4514-8968-2

The paper used in this publication meets the minimum requirements of American National Standard for Information Sciences — Permanence of Paper for Printed Library Materials, ANSI Z329.48-1984.

Manufactured in the U.S.A.

This book was produced using PressBooks.com, and PDF rendering was done by PrinceXML.

Contents

Introduction

I was glad when Fortress Press decided to issue an abbreviated version of my book, *Histories of the Latin American Church: A Handbook*. The original text, while a labor of love and passion, could be considered too unwieldy for the casual student curious about Christianity in Latin America. Its detailed treatment of over twenty countries, their chronologies, popular devotions, and eminent personalities make up the bulk of that particular project. This *Brief Introduction* is essentially the first part of that larger work: general essays on history and theology, basic information on religious traditions, and a few sections culled from the appendix. It is designed to serve as a more manageable introduction to the topic for undergraduates, seminary students, and curious onlookers wishing for a bird's-eye view. For those who want to come down from the heights and pursue a more in-depth journey throughout the individual countries that make up modern Latin America, the larger volume is to be preferred.

Within the last twenty years there has been a renewed attention to the many expressions of Christianity around the world. Church history texts that begin in Palestine, travel through Europe, and then culminate in the United States are no longer acceptable in the college or graduate classroom, and indeed they should not be. The Internet, to a great extent, has helped facilitate the interest in world

Christianity, not only in the resources available and the personal connections individuals make but in the daily news. Just this year, Arab populations have tried to alert the West of the violence being suffered by millennia-old Christian communities in Syria and Egypt, and in parts of Africa legislators debate the passage of draconian laws against sexual minorities drafted with the support of evangelical churches from both there and the United States. As one of the most densely populated regions of the world with civilizations dating back thousands of years and some of the strongest emerging economies looking forward, Latin America can no longer be relegated to a secondary role in global affairs. Similarly, Latin American Christianity stands poised to play an even greater part in the future of the faith worldwide. It is both Western and global, heir to European, African, and indigenous theologies, worldviews, and spiritualities. It was postcolonial before that became "a thing." Its Pentecostal churches send missionaries around the world, and one of her sons now sits upon the papal throne as head of the Roman Catholic Church. No religion, including Christianity, is monolithic. Whether one is a believer or not, Christian traditions are products of cultures and worldviews interacting with one another. The "great traditions" of denominations and dominant powers and the "little traditions" of local customs and observances collide, collude, and come together within larger cultural contexts to create varieties of faith and devotion. For the Christian, this is to be expected and valued being that Christianity itself begins with the story of incarnation within a particular people, place, and time.

In roughly the last two centuries, the meaning of "Latin America" has been debated again and again. There are several popular uses of the term:

Geographic: For many, especially in the United States, the name refers to everything south of the US border, including the parts of the region that speak English (Belize, Bermuda, Grenada, Barbados), French (Haiti, Martinique), and Dutch (Suriname). The historic and cultural differences make this definition too broad for our use.

Linguistic: Strictly speaking, this would point to all regions in the Americas that use a Romance language. It was in this sense that the French sought to make allies of the Ibero-American countries in the nineteenth century to counter the political and economic weight of Anglo-America and Teutonic Europe. While narrower than the usage above, it is still too broad, forcing one to include not only Haiti and Guadeloupe, but also French-speaking Quebec.

Historical/Cultural: These are the regions that have been united by a common historical experience of Iberian conquest, colonization, and nineteenth-century independence movements, which were then followed by a period of populist regimes and civil wars until the present time. This is the definition used in this book. It is identical to Ibero-America but with the important caveat that the region's cultural identity cannot be defined solely by Spanish and Portuguese domination; Amerindian and African elements have been equal components (all in various combinations in various proportions) in the formation of a new cultural identity that is more than the sum of its parts. It is a cultural mélange to which are constantly added new elements: Italian, German, Japanese, Arab, and Korean, among others. Under this banner, I also include the Latin American diaspora in the United States. The migration of Mexicans, Cubans, and Central Americans into the United States, as well as the movement of the US border over parts of what were once Mexico and the Spanish Empire, has resulted in a continuity of culture that transcends political boundaries. Add to this the fact that the United States is the fifth largest Spanish-speaking country in world and one has further reason to include it within our definition.

Readers will note that I use the terms *Hispanic* and *Latino* interchangeably to describe the populations in the United States that have their roots in the cultures and histories of Latin America. I do so to avoid repetition, aware that the terms carry certain sociopolitical connotations. The same goes for the words *indigenous, native, Indian,* or *Amerindian* used to designate the people living on this continent before European contact. Because dates, events, and narratives have sometimes been conflicting, absent, or difficult to ascertain, I have tried to reconstruct them to the best of my ability. Any errors or omissions contained herein are strictly my responsibility.

This book you hold in your hands (and its heavier incarnation) has been my constant companion for well over a year now since inception. The trials, hopes, visions, and tears of a continent have informed and enlightened my own perspectives of the Christian religion not only there, but as I explore the faith in the United States and elsewhere. These very same stories of human failing and human potential have grieved and energized my soul. In addition to assisting readers in their research I hope it will also lead them to appreciate the beauty and color of a people in this sun-kissed region. On this level as well I hope this book serves as a guide to fellow Hispanics seeking to recover a past too often ignored by the churches and the academy. In the words of the Brazilian Protestant theologian Rubem Alves:

> The historian is someone who recovers lost memories and distributes them as a sacrament to those who have lost the memories. Indeed, what finer communal sacrament is there than the memories of a common past,

punctuated by the existence of pain, sacrifice and hope? To recover in order to disperse. The historian is not an archaeologist of memories. The historian is a sower of visions and hopes.

This work would have been impossible without the gentle guidance and support of Will Bergkamp, Lisa Gruenisen, and the team at Fortress Press who have allowed me this small contribution to academia. I continue to be indebted to my teachers, whose voices linger and inform my efforts. The congregation at Holy Trinity Lutheran Church in Chicago has accompanied me through times of joy and struggle; in their encouragement, their ministry has challenged me to step out of the comfort of the mythical ivory tower. This is the point where one would say a few sentimental words of thanks for one's spouse or significant other. Seeing as that is not possible, I will continue to be grateful for the endless well of faith and support that is my mother, Eva. She taught me to pray in Spanish when I was four and, decades later, continues to remind me that faith must be a matter of the heart and hands as well as the head. Besides, what kind of Latin boy would I be if I did not acknowledge my *mamita*? Finally, for the companionship of dogs, demanding to play on a summer afternoon or curled at my feet on a polar vortex night, good Lord, we give thanks.

Joel Morales Cruz
Commemoration of Bartolomé de Las Casas, 2014

1

Christianity in Latin America

A Short History

1:1: Prologue

Latin America unites in itself the European, African, and American streams of civilization. Similarly so, Christianity did not develop in an airtight, pasteurized package but was influenced by the religions and worldviews of the cultures in which it took root.

1:1:1: The Iberian Background

Spain and Portugal on the cusp of the age of exploration were the result of centuries of struggle between the emerging Christian kingdoms in the north and the Muslims in the south of the peninsula, known as Al-Andalus. Conquered in 711 by Arab and Berber forces, Al-Andalus became a center of learning, art, poetry, industry, and, to a certain extent, tolerance toward Christians and Jews; for the latter, such tolerance was unknown in the rest of Europe. As the

Islamic caliphate splintered into smaller, independent, but weaker *taifas*, Christian rulers pushed southward in the Reconquista. By the time that Isabel of Castile and Fernando of Aragon conquered the last-standing Muslim kingdom of Granada in 1492, Spain was enthralled to myths of divine election for the preservation and expansion of Christianity, which was accompanied by a militant Catholicism, already in the process of reforming itself and intolerant of any vestige of unorthodoxy, let alone other religions.

Royal Patronage

Known as the *patronato real* in Spain and the *padroado real* in neighboring Portugal, the royal patronage consisted of the right to name bishops to empty offices. Throughout the Middle Ages it was long debated who rightfully held that privilege, the pope by virtue of being the vicar of Christ or the secular ruler for his support, financial and otherwise, of the church's mission within the realm. Was this power inherent in the right to rule or was it a privilege given and revoked by the See of Peter? What was clear was that whoever named the bishops effectively controlled the church. In a series of papal bulls in the late fifteenth century, the privilege was ceded to the Catholic monarchs over whatever territories they came to by conquest or discovery. By the reign of Philip II (1554–1598), Spain would effectively rule over the Latin American church through the selection of bishops, the calling of councils, the implementation of policy, and control over communication between the Vatican and the dioceses. To this union of altar and throne one can add the Spanish Inquisition, begun in 1478 and solely under the control of the monarchs, as a means of establishing orthodoxy, morality, and submission. It would be an invigorated, zealous, and state-controlled

Catholicism, convinced of Spain's manifest destiny in the face of false religions, that would come to be planted in the New World.

1:1:2: African Cosmologies

The people who were forcibly removed to the Americas from the sixteenth through the nineteenth centuries came from a number of politically and culturally sophisticated kingdoms of West Africa, among them the Yoruba, Bantu, Fon-Ewe, and Kongo. Their religious worldviews included belief in a supreme deity—Olodumaré (Yoruba), Nazambi Kalunga (Kongo), or Onyankopon (Akan)—who rules the universe through hundreds of lesser gods, spirits, and ancestors. In general, worship and sacrifice are offered to these beings in order to appease them, bring health, ask for favors, divine the future, or restore harmony to the world. Among the Yoruba, whose religious influence is especially pronounced in Afro-Latin religions, the individual spirits (*orishas*) hold sway over particular spheres of influence (iron tools, storms, disease, and so on). Through ritual dancing, offerings, and the aid of a medium, the *orishas* make their desires known in spirit possession. In some groups, ritualized objects can be used to bind and control the spirits. The goal of human life is to collect *ashe*, or power—the same that energizes the spirits and runs through the cosmos—while maintaining ordered relationships toward other people, the ancestors, and the spirits.

1:1:3: Amerindian Religion

The American continent was populated by people who began to enter it over the Bering Strait (and possibly over the Pacific Ocean) in waves of migration that began between fifteen and twenty-five thousand years ago. They developed into a myriad of people groups with a diversity of cultures and languages unknown in the Old World and whose civilizations ranged from nomadic hunter-gatherers to the Maya, Aztec, and Inca empire builders. Brazil alone had fourteen hundred distinct peoples and forty linguistic families. Similarly, their religious worldviews defy easy generalizations. Some aspects of indigenous spirituality include the intersection between sacred time, place, and human life. Deeply connected to the rhythms of nature, the seasons, and the stars, time was seen as cyclical and creation as a continual process of birth, life, death, and rebirth. Story and ritual connect humanity to the forces of nature, which are often theomorphized into spirits and gods. Space, time, humanity, and the gods are seen as interdependent. The gods may create, sustain, and renew the cosmos but are in need of sustenance and appeasement through sacrifice, which may take forms such as feathers and butterflies, ritual bloodletting, or, as in the case of the Aztecs, human lives. A cosmic harmony would be the outcome of this give-and-take relationship between people, gods, nature, time, and space.

For the two great powers that the Spanish encountered, the Aztec and the Inca, religion served as an ideological prop to their expansion, interweaving with social, military, and economic might to justify their control over broad swaths of the continent. The Aztecs incorporated their history into the mythologies of previous civilizations in order to legitimize their rule. Tezcatlipoca and Huitzilopochtli, gods of war, served as patron deities for the capital city of Tenochtitlán (present-day Mexico City). Continuous sacrifice in their honor would serve to guarantee not only the future of Aztec military success but also the stability of creation. Meanwhile, the Inca, ruling from the sacred city of Cuzco, held to Virachocha, the creator, and to Inti, the sun, in addition to numerous minor deities and spirits. The royal family was considered to be descended from the sun, thus making the emperor, *the* Inca, semidivine. Upon the emperors' deaths, their mummified remains (*huacas*) were venerated. As the Inca empire expanded, the worship of Inti was grafted onto the religion of the conquered peoples, who were expected to give the sun god preeminence of sacrifice. This, of course, served as a daily reminder of their subjugation under the children of the sun.

1:2: Christianity in Conquest and Colonization (1492–1810)

The planting of Christianity in the Americas was an endeavor of both imperialist greed and evangelical self-sacrifice. As Christian institutions and spiritualities developed in Latin America, they took on forms and emphases that continue to inform faith and practice today.

1:2:1: Cross and Sword

Christopher Columbus sailed forth in search of a back door to the wealth of Asia, convinced of a divine mandate to take Christianity to whatever lands he encountered and to return with the means for a final crusade to liberate the Holy Land from Islam. He encountered more than what he bargained for, and his exploratory successors quickly determined that this was a New World filled with people, cultures, tongues, flora, and fauna never before known to any Europeans. In the meantime, Pope Alexander VI in 1494 divided these "discoveries," potential or real, between the Spanish and the Portuguese in the Treaty of Tordesillas. A year earlier, the papal bull *Inter caetera* had admonished the Spanish sovereigns to spread the Christian faith wherever they went.

As the Spanish ventured further into the West Indies and eventually the mainland, they encountered new civilizations. At first, they thought that these people did not hold any religious beliefs, seeing as they did not worship in ways recognizable to Europeans. However, as they came face-to-face with the intricate mythologies and religious systems of the Maya and the Aztec, they concluded that these natives worshipped some sort of Satanically-inspired false gods. The blood-soaked altars of the temples in Tenochtitlán that Cortéz witnessed in 1519 did not help. Reactions varied. Some conquistadors, using interpreters or rudimentary signs, sought to convince the rulers to abandon their gods and accept Baptism. To the Spanish, this implied vassalage to the king of Spain. To the Indians, the Spanish were potential and powerful allies against their enemies. Other conquistadors, in horror and shock of the "idols" and accompanying rituals, would tear down the altars. In either case, whether by cajoling or by force, the images of Mary and the cross would replace the traditional deities atop the sacred sites and the native priests commended to care for them. As the Europeans gained victory after victory through force of arms and force of germs, the appropriation of indigenous temples by Christian symbols would carry an additional message: the defeat of the old gods and the rise of the new world order.

Religious Justification for Conquest

The existence of a new continent peopled by hitherto-unknown civilizations posed a conundrum to the Spanish. How could a new world even exist that had not been mentioned in the Bible? How could it be reconciled with the Genesis stories of creation, the flood, and the disbursement of the nations? Were these new people fully human? Did they possess souls? Their cultures, social customs, and religions were so foreign as to create doubt in the European mind as to their faculties of reason, morality, and humanity. Even though Pope Paul III declared the Indians to be fully human in *Sublimus Deus*, the matter was not fully settled. These questions were framed within both the economic context of the conquests—namely, the expectation that the colonies would produce wealth for the royal treasury—and the philosophical framework in which theological reflection was being done. According to Aristotle's *Politics*, some people (and nations) are meant to rule over others who, by nature, are inferior and/or destined for slavery. This was the argument presented by theologians such as Juan Gínes de Sepúlveda. It spelled forth the prerogatives of empire while justifying the violent and cruel treatment of the Indians, already in the process of being decimated by slavery and disease. One of Sepúlveda's contemporaries, Francisco de Vitoria, proposed a universal law of nations wherein all people were fully human, could attain salvation, and possessed an inherent right to their lives and property. In this instance, the Spanish would have to possess the legal right to deprive the Indians of their lands, as in the case of a just war. Francisco Pizarro's attack on Atahualpa, the Inca ruler, in response to his desecration of a breviary can be seen in such a light. More significantly, the establishment in 1513 of the Requerimiento, a document to be read aloud placing the discovered lands under Spanish rule and demanding submission to the throne and the acceptance of Christianity, provided the legal cover to declare a just war, even when proclaimed without an interpreter or read aloud to empty beaches.

Resistance

Though individual priests or friars accompanied the first voyages of exploration to minister to the Spanish, it would not be until 1510 that members of the religious orders arrived in the New World for the express purpose of evangelizing the Indians. Friars of the Dominican Order were the first to the island of Hispaniola and while, throughout history, many clerics would subscribe to and benefit from the imperial theology, these newcomers quickly decided they would not. Led by Pedro de Córdoba, they became the first voices of conscience in the New World. The fiery Advent sermon of Antonio de Montesinos questioned the Christianity of the settlers in light of their exploitation of and cruelty to the Indians. In his audience was a young priest, Bartolomé de Las Casas, who himself held an *encomienda*, or grant of Indians, to work his farm. After being present at the brutal and bloody conquest of Cuba he would have a change of heart in 1514 and dedicate the rest of his life to bringing justice to the Indians. Becoming a Dominican himself, he would crisscross the ocean several times to present the natives' case before the king. The New Laws of 1542 abolishing the *encomienda* were the result, although they were enforced only temporarily. Las Casas defended the full humanity and dignity of the Amerindians in debate with Sepúlveda in 1550, and he propounded a revolutionary theory in missions, arguing that the only way to spread the gospel was through peace, persuasion, and love. Though a child of his era and ever seeking to reconcile the rights of the indigenous with the expanding Spanish empire, he could on his deathbed only see the judgment of God upon Spain for the death they visited upon the Indians. Others, though lesser known, would strive to resist the power of the sword. For example, Bishop Antonio de Valdivieso of Nicaragua was assassinated by the colonists for his defense of the Indians and Vasco de Quiroga, bishop of Michoacán in Mexico, sought to separate the native peoples under his charge from the Spanish and create a peaceful community inspired by Thomas More's *Utopia*.

Yet just as violence takes on more than simply physical forms, so does resistance. Cultural decimation was faced by the native peoples as missionaries upended their religious rituals, destroyed their sacred books and artifacts, and dismissed and attacked their belief systems and mores as demonic. Franciscan missionary Bernardo de Sahagún was one of the few who sought to preserve the Aztec past in codices and histories. Yet others went further to vindicate the indigenous worldview within the Christian faith now dominant. Blas Valera, a sixteenth-century mestizo Jesuit, was disciplined for daring to suggest that Inca religion and culture were the equal of Christianity. In the early seventeenth century, Guaman Poma de Ayala, born of Indian royalty, penned a lengthy tome addressed to Phillip III seeking justice from the abuses of the Spanish and arguing that the religion of his Inca ancestors was compatible with the Christian faith. The rebellion led by Túpac Amaru II in Peru in 1778 sought to overthrow the Spanish in the hope of establishing Christian Inca rule.

1:2:2: Expanding the Church

Having encountered a "new" continent and "new" civilizations, the Catholic Church desired to bring people to the faith and establish itself within American society. Yet even in the New World, old habits die hard.

Evangelization

The task of evangelization fell mainly to the members of religious orders (whereas secular clergy were more concentrated in urban areas and ministered to the colonists and others within the diocesan system). Dominicans, Franciscans, Jesuits, and Augustinians were the earliest and most numerous of the orders. In the early part of the colonial period, friars learned the Indian languages, often being the first to put them into written form and to create grammars and dictionaries. Not only were these valuable for those missionaries setting forth to work among the natives, but they have enabled future generations of linguists to study the development and preservation of these languages. Catechetical instruction often used pictograms, as well as the natural drama of the Mass, sermons, music, and religious theater. Early on, schools were established in Mexico to train the children of Indian nobles to be priests, but eventually those efforts were suspended due to prejudice. However similar some of the orders' tools were, often their perspectives and methodologies varied. Franciscans had been highly influenced by the apocalyptic visions of medieval teacher Joachim of Fiore. They came to believe that the "discovery" of a New World heralded the end of days and hurried to bring as many into the kingdom of heaven as possible. As a result they tended to baptize first and catechize later. Dominicans, the Order of Preachers, took the opposite approach, focusing on teaching the natives the rudiments of the Christian faith and practice first. These differences led to clashes between the orders in areas where their ministries overlapped. Franciscans, Jesuits, and to a lesser extent Dominicans also took part in the *congregaciones*—that is, the removal of nomadic or scattered Indian groups into protected villages. This served several purposes: it facilitated evangelism by having the people in one place; it separated the natives from the predations or the influence of the Spanish, who were considered bad examples; and, finally, it removed them from their traditional lifestyles, lands, and practices in order to "civilize" them into farming, manufacture, and trade as well as Christian faith. The most famous of these were the Jesuit reductions of the seventeenth and eighteenth centuries in what are now Paraguay, Brazil, and northern Argentina. The Jesuit attitude toward indigenous lifestyles was more sympathetic than those of the other orders or the diocesan church. Though often paternalistic, the Jesuits tried to maintain traditional social and political structures as much as possible. In removing the Guaraní from their seminomadic lifestyles, the *reducciones* have been criticized as an example of cultural violation. However, they also served to protect them from Portuguese slave-raiders. The independence of the order, and consequently its mission, enraged and terrified colonists fearful that the Jesuits were raising an army. The economic success of the missions through their agriculture, livestock, artisanship, and manufacturing was yet another reason for colonial envy. After the Guaraní War of 1756 and the subsequent expulsion of the Society of Jesus in the 1760s, the reductions were eventually abandoned.

The situation in Brazil differed in that the Portuguese did not set out to build colonies as the Spanish did but to establish trading posts along the coast as they had done in Africa in order to exploit the area's resources. Not until the latter half of the fifteenth century was any effort put into establishing permanent settlements devoted to sugar production. It was then that the king, under the powers of the *padroado*, favored the Society of Jesus to serve as the chief agents of evangelization. The Jesuit method of congregating Indians into missions for the purposes of evangelization and acculturation, however, had the effect of removing them from the Portuguese labor force, enraging both colonists and some members of the secular clergy.

Consolidation

Universalis Ecclesiae Regimen, a papal bull issued by Pope Julius II in 1508, granted the Spanish monarchs full rights of patronage over the church in the "Indies." This allowed Fernando, and Charles I after him, to establish dioceses and supervise the development of the American church with the aid of the Council of the Indies in Seville. Santo Domingo was the first diocese created, originally under the archdiocese of Seville until 1546 when it was elevated in rank. By 1620 more than thirty dioceses dotted the New World. Santo Domingo, Mexico, Lima, Charcas de la Plata, Bogotá, and Buenos Aires served as archdioceses in the urban centers of the Spanish viceroyalties and important provinces. Already by midcentury, the archbishops of Mexico and Lima, representing the viceroyalties of New Spain and Peru, began to call forth provincial councils to organize the task of evangelism, standards for the clergy, and the consolidation of the diocesan structure. In the 1570s and 1580s, the bishops, in particular Toribio de Mogrovejo of Lima, began implementing the decrees of the Council of Trent, resulting in a more bureaucratic and structured church. Both the religious orders and the secular church established universities and hospitals for the minds and bodies of the colonists. The first printing presses were introduced in order to produce catechisms, books, and devotional literature for their edification. Women's religious orders began to increase in number, and the Inquisition in New Spain and Peru arrived to root out heresy and immoral behavior.

1:2:3: The Colonial Church

The colonial church was one of the central pillars of Iberian society. Its power and influence were felt throughout all levels from the religious to the economic to the social. Its spirit and influence continue to reverberate across the continent in its churches, its piety, and its worldview.

Age of the Baroque

Baroque Christianity posited a world where the sacred was profoundly immanent. There was little distinction between a symbol and the thing signified. Therefore, the divine was both material and reachable through the senses. Post-Tridentine Catholicism, both in Europe and in the Americas, emphasized the role of emotion drawn forth by art and liturgy. Opulent churches, particularly in rich urban centers like Lima, Cuzco, Puebla, and Mexico City, sought to draw the eye ever upward in awe and contemplation of God triumphant in the church and the world. Elaborate liturgies and festival celebrations, entertaining sight, sound, smell, and hearing, were used to inspire and reinforce social structures. The Corpus Christi processionals, for example, not only commemorated the body of Christ present in the Eucharist but also underlined the established body politic by mirroring the social hierarchy. Everyone in their place and a place for everyone. Confraternities, imported from Spain and Portugal, established smaller communities based on race or occupation under the patronage of a favored saint. These brotherhoods—part union, part welfare, and part funeral insurance—performed charitable works and sponsored religious festivals, fortifying social connections under the auspices of heaven. On a more personal scale, the immediacy and palpability of the divine meant that, for the believer, miracles and healing could be as close as the nearest relic, holy site, or mystic. The cult of saints, the friends of Christ and benefactors of the devout, were among the most intimate of intermediaries between the human and divine in reflection of the imperial order. Lavish gifts, whether to the image of a saint or to the functioning of a Mass, were seen as visible signs of one's devotion. This sense of physicality, immanence, and relationship with the sacred through pilgrimage, emotion, offering, and sacrifice dovetailed with indigenous and African spirituality and symbolism, which in turn made themselves known in the art, architecture, and popular religion of the era.

Popular Religion

Popular religion—that is, the beliefs and rituals of the masses—developed strongly in Latin America for a number of reasons: the lack of clergy available to sufficiently catechize isolated groups, the false assumption that people came to Christianity with a tabula rasa devoid of their own religious worldviews, the retention or adaptation of previous religious beliefs as a form of resistance to the colonists, and the fact that many clerics preferred to work with the European population and paid scant attention to the needs of the indigenous or, more often, the Africans. Popular religiosity in Latin America often reflected colonial society itself, a combination of European, African, and American elements into something new. In these creative variations to Christianity, the native and the African were placed on par with the European. The Virgin of Guadalupe, appearing to Juan Diego Cuauhtlatoatzin in 1531, appeared as a dark-skinned Indian and used Nahua religious symbols and terminology to proclaim acceptance to the Indians. Black Christs were not only popular among the Central American Maya for whom the color carried religious meaning, including death and rebirth, but also among African populations in South America who saw the Christian God as identifying with their skin color and pain. Along Lake Titicaca, the Virgin of Copacabana became identified with the Earth Mother and, like the Pachamama, is called upon even today in times of harvest.

Women

Women generally had two proper places in colonial society: in the home or in the convent. Until the seventeenth century the church generally favored individual choice in marriage, giving shelter and performing marriages even when parents disapproved of the union. Wealthier women entered marriage with a dowry, giving them some degree of independence and allowing them to become benefactors of churches or charities. Convent life varied from the strictly observant to the lax, from the simple to the extravagant. Women of well-to-do families entered the religious life with dowries as well, which in some cases were invested, allowing convents to become prosperous landowners or to serve as essential lending institutions in the city. (Unlike men's religious houses, which were generally rural, convents were urban and, in the case of wealthy ones, could span several city blocks.)

Though the life of a religious could be heavily regulated, some found it to be an avenue for expression, independence, and even rebellion in the absence of a husband. The spiritual autobiography, usually written by mystics under the supervision of a confessor priest, is a genre that afforded women self-expression and allowed them to voice sometimes unconventional opinions directly or indirectly. Sometimes though, as in the case of Catarina de San Juan in Mexico, it could provoke the scrutiny of the Inquisition. The Hieronymite convent in Mexico City, however, afforded women more freedom. Those with some degree of wealth owned private cells, retained property, and entered the convent with slaves. Here, the seventeenth-century polymath Sor Juana Inés de la Cruz found the liberty to write poetry and drama, and even to defend a woman's right to study theology. There were some women who defied convention. Catalina de Erauso went to war disguised as a man before being discovered and sent to a convent. After escaping, she successfully petitioned the pope to allow her to continue living under a male identity. In the mid-1700s, Rosa Egipcíaca was a former prostitute and slave whose mystic experiences made her the first black woman to be published in Brazil before her controversial visions and rituals led to her judgment by the Inquisition in Portugal. A century earlier, the young mystic Rosa de Lima refused marriage and lived a severe, ascetic life as a Third Order Dominican in her parents' house before becoming the Americas' first canonized saint.

Africans

Slavery was introduced into the Spanish and Portuguese colonies largely as a result of the decimation of the Indian population and subsequent legal protections against their exploitation. In general, the institution, accepted throughout the Mediterranean world, was never questioned. The church and the religious orders, especially the Jesuits, availed themselves of slave labor to work their estates, colleges, and missions. Concentrated in the Caribbean and Brazil, the church engaged in no concentrated evangelistic outreach toward the Africans. The efforts of Alonso de Sandoval and Pedro Claver in Colombia are the exceptions that prove the rule. Oftentimes Africans were baptized as they were led aboard the Portuguese slave ships or upon disembarking. In Brazil, plantation owners were held responsible for the religious instruction of their slaves, which was conducted not by catechesis but through exposure to the prayers, festivals, and rhythms of the Mass and the church calendar in the plantation chapel or local church. Slaves and free blacks formed brotherhoods for mutual support under the patronage of a saint. Blacks and mixed-race people were generally not permitted in the priesthood or religious orders but could serve as *donados*, living under the monastic rules but working as servants. Martín de Porres of Peru was such a *donado* until later in life when the Dominican friary in which he lived permitted him full orders as the result of his reputation for sanctity, piety, and miracles. In the early nineteenth century, José Nunes Garcia was ordained to the priesthood and achieved prominence as a musician in Brazil despite racial prejudice and opposition.

A lack of religious instruction, the high mortality rate of blacks necessitating a steady influx of new slaves, and the determination to maintain their culture and religion led many Afro-Latin communities to adapt their religious customs. Combining elements and practices from Catholicism and traditional religions, Santería, Candomblé, and Palo Monte were often practiced in secret so as not to arouse suspicion. These and other Afro-Latin religions became a source of resilience for many black communities and have since drawn adherents from all colors and classes.

The Catholic Enlightenment

The Bourbon Reforms enacted by the kings of Spain in the eighteenth century were designed to increase the wealth returning from the American colonies and to centralize power, including that of the church, in the monarchy. Charles III was especially interested in improving the state of the church and the educational levels of the clergy in both Spain and its colonies. Naturally, he appointed bishops sympathetic to his goals. The Catholic Enlightenment, both in Europe and abroad, was an effort to reconcile rationalism with revelation, to pursue Enlightenment thought in science, politics, philosophy, and theology without abandoning Catholic orthodoxy. In the Americas, enlightened bishops revisited university curricula, exchanging Aristotle for the natural sciences. As a result, knowledge of the continent's geography, flora, and fauna were enhanced, as were astronomical observations. In the life of the church, the extravagant adornment of the churches and images of the saints were discouraged in favor of works of charity. Preachers were admonished to cease obsequious, Latin-ridden sermons and to speak plainly for the spiritual edification of the people. Popular religious festivals became highly regulated or even suspended out of concern for immorality as well as to stem attitudes and practices now considered "superstitious." The emphasis on the saints and their devotion was downplayed; instead, clerics were encouraged to emphasize the Bible, Christ, and his presence in the Eucharist.

One distinctly New World effect of the Catholic Enlightenment was a consciousness of American identity and pride among American-born Spaniards in response to European prejudices. Considered inferior or unreliable for having been born in the colonies, Creoles were often denied access to the highest positions of society in favor of the European-born. A renewed interest in the natural sciences led to an appreciation of the New World's resources. Some, including churchmen, began investigating the indigenous civilizations of the past and comparing them favorably to the civilizations of Greece or Rome. The old question about the role of the Americas in salvation history came back to life in light of similarities between indigenous religions and Christianity, with some theorizing that the hero-god Quetzalcoatl must have actually been the apostle Thomas bringing the gospel to the Americas long before the Spanish arrived. Others pointed to the miraculous Marian apparitions as proof of God's providential favor on these shores. Whatever the argument, the results were jaw-dropping. If the Christian message was introduced to the New World by a first-century apostle or the Virgin Mary herself, what justification was there for the conquest and colonization of the Americas? And if God had so blessed these lands, then who is to say that its citizens are second-class and unfit to rule them?

1:3: Christianity and the Independent Republics (1810–1930)

As the Spanish and Portuguese colonies struggled toward self-determination, the church endeavored to maintain its influence, oppose the challenges of Protestantism and secularism, and define its place on the continent.

1:3:1: Insurrection in God's Name

Most of Latin America, with the exceptions of Brazil, Cuba, and Puerto Rico, began shaking off European rule at the beginning off the nineteenth century. In many places throughout the colonies, from Mexico to Argentina, parish priests led or joined the insurrections. Most were Creole or mixed-race and so identified with their native lands and the people they served rather than faraway Spain. Many were well-read in the Enlightenment thinkers of the age, including Rousseau and Locke. Napoleon's invasion of Spain in 1808 and the overthrow of Fernando VII presented the opportunity to rebel. The insurrectionists based their actions on the natural right of freedom for human beings and on a continued allegiance to the rightful Spanish king. With very few exceptions, the bishops opposed the independence movements. For one, most were European-born Spaniards, and all owed their positions to the Spanish throne. Secondly, of course, was the traditional antipathy for rebellion against the divine right of kings. As the battles for independence waged back and forth across the several arenas of the continent, religious symbolism and coercion were used to rally the contestants. In Mexico, the Dark Virgin, Guadalupe, flew on the standards of the rebels while the royalists clung to the Virgin of Remedies who had accompanied Cortéz into conquest three centuries prior. Colombian priest and later bishop of Bogotá Juan Fernández de Sotomayor authored a catechism describing the revolution as holy and just. At the same time, Our Lady of Mercies was declared patron of the Argentine army, and in Uruguay in 1825, the Thirty-Three, patriot heroes against then-Brazilian rule, swore fidelity to the Virgin now known by their name. The bishops thundered excommunication and anathema against the rebels but to no avail. In the end, many of them fled to Spain, creating an ecclesiastical crisis of authority for the new republics.

Brazil's road to independence struck a different path. As Napoleon's forces marched towards Portugal, the royal court fled to Brazil, elevating it from colony to kingdom upon their arrival. The Brazilian church benefited from their presence and investment. In 1817 the failed Pernambucan Revolt against the Portuguese Court included fifty-seven liberal priests. However, on King João VI's return to Portugal in 1822, the prince, Pedro, declared Brazilian independence with the full cooperation of the church. Under a legitimate ruler of the royal house, there was no danger of the sin of rebellion.

1:3:2: Church and State

By the mid-1820s, the colonies of Latin America had achieved independence. Several nations sought to unite under a single banner, creating the Federal Republic of Central America and Gran Colombia, but political divisions between their component parts doomed this effort early on. With regard to the Catholic Church, several issues were immediately at hand. To the relief of the church, practically every one of the new independent states acknowledged the central role of the Catholic Church, guaranteeing it a spiritual monopoly in their early constitutions (along with control of education and the civil registry) with very few voices offering support for freedom of conscience at this early stage. The next major crisis for the church was the *patronato*. Namely, did the right to appoint bishops to vacant sees revert back to Rome upon the sundering of royal rule or did the governments of the new nations inherit it? The result was a tug of war between the Americas and the papacy with the fate of the Catholic Church at hand. Many bishops, loyal to the Spanish throne, had fled across the Atlantic, and in several cases they were exiled for their lack of patriotic support to the nationalist cause. Considering that he who controlled the bishops controlled the church—the largest landowner, a repository of wealth and knowledge, and a voice of influence throughout the continent, the stakes were high indeed. The Vatican at first refused to recognize the independent states and did not begin to do so until after the death of Fernando VI, the Spanish king, in 1833. This alone hampered the recognition of national patronage. By midcentury, many countries had hammered out concordats with Rome, each side trying to reap the lion's share of benefits. Most usually, these agreements allowed the Catholic Church to remain the official religion of the state, to retain its properties and traditional privileges (ecclesiastical courts, collection of the tithe), and to control the registry of births and deaths and the system of education. In return, the papacy would recognize the government's right to choose and present nominees to vacant dioceses. As the century wore on, many of the concordats were broken or dissolved as national governments instituted liberal freedoms or abrogated terms of agreement. In a few countries, the agreements were revisited and renegotiated and remain in place, as in Venezuela.

Conservatives and Liberals

Behind these struggles to negotiate the role of the Catholic Church in the independent republics lay battles over the very nature of these countries. Throughout most of Latin America, two major groups, led by the landed, white elite, emerged in the 1820s. Conservatives sought a system of government that would retain as much of the colonial structure as possible, including the centrality of the church. Liberals looked to a federal form of government along with the institution of modern freedoms and reforms such as liberty of conscience and secular education. The church, weakened by a lack of priests and bishops, the persecution of religious orders, and the destruction or elimination of many of its schools, libraries, and seminaries during the emancipation process, was seemingly caught in the middle. Both parties sought to control the church to their own ends, one by using it as an arm of the state and the other by undermining its powers. Anticlerical elements existed among both, even while paying lip service to the church. Faithful Catholics existed among both, even if that meant a Catholicism adapted to the modern world. The fortunes of the church often swung back and forth as the political winds blew. In general, church leaders sided with the Conservatives well into the twentieth century. Under Liberal rule, the bishops saw their power diminished. As the century progressed, Catholicism was forced to adapt to new circumstances. No longer a powerful state church, it grudgingly had to contend with the modern challenge to the model of Christendom as, in various degrees, country after country began to experiment with freedom of conscience and even separation of church and state.

1:3:3: First Protestants

The cultural, philosophical, and religious context of Latin American independence was different from that of the religiously pluralistic English colonies to the north. Ideas of freedom did not translate into equal civil rights for all. In general, with independence the Iberian colonies had traded one oligarchic rule for another. Freedom of religion was barely a blip on the radar for most of the region's leaders. Eventually, liberty of conscience was enacted throughout the various republics as a practical solution to the challenge of stimulating economic and political relationships with other countries. Whereas the occasional unfortunate Protestant would wash up on shore during the colonial period, Protestantism as a whole did not begin entering Latin America until after independence. Some of the first Protestants were members of Bible societies and Bible colporteurs whose goal was to spread the knowledge of the Scriptures. The most famous and peripatetic of these was James "Diego" Thompson, a Scotsman who traveled from Argentina to Mexico to the Caribbean, often at the invitation of political leaders and with the support of some of the Catholic hierarchy and clergy. In some circles, the Bible and Protestantism were seen as the key to the economic and political success of Great Britain and the United States; to gain parity with those nations meant introducing those pillars of Anglo-American power. Echoing the Enlightenment Catholics of the prior century, they believed that ignorance and religious superstition were causes of Latin American stagnation. In several countries religious freedom was extended only to foreigners, and chaplains arrived soon afterward to serve them and in some cases extended their ministries to the surrounding population. As religious liberty was promulgated throughout the republics, missionaries, primarily from the United States, came. To grasp the beginnings of the Protestant missions, it is important to understand their context—namely, a triumphalist, postmillennial revivalist evangelicalism that existed within the larger framework of US economic and political expansionism inspired by convictions of Manifest Destiny. This was especially apparent after 1898 when Spain lost Puerto Rico and Cuba in the Spanish-American War and the major Protestant denominations divided up the islands between themselves to establish churches and save people from Roman Catholicism. Methodist, Presbyterian, Baptist, Congregationalist, Episcopal, and Lutheran missionaries generally began working among the poor and laborers but soon began to concentrate on the emerging middle classes who tended to be more critical of Roman Catholic clericalism and would be more receptive to the republican values the missionaries espoused. In some areas, such as Mexico City, the missionaries worked among reformist clergy and religious groups. Nascent congregations built churches, schools, clinics, seminaries, and other charitable institutions. At this stage, though, the US missionary enterprise tended toward paternalism and sometimes outright prejudice. Despite the development of native leaders, the missionaries and the denominations they represented maintained control.

Another source for the Protestant presence in Latin America lay in national efforts to stimulate industry by inviting immigrant groups to settle underpopulated areas. German Mennonites arrived in Argentina, Paraguay, and Uruguay while their Russian counterparts settled in northern Mexico. Italian Waldensians also found new homes in the Southern Cone. Until later in the twentieth century, these communities tended to be isolated, forming their own churches and hiring pastors from abroad. Only later, as the second and third generations identified more with the New World than the Old, were services and ministries formed that also extended outward.

1:3:4: At Century's End

In the late nineteenth century, throughout parts of Latin America, the Catholic Church had to contend with several Liberal regimes ruled by powerful *caudillos*. Their approach to the church varied from the relatively benign, such as in Porfirio Díaz's Mexico where he allowed the church to regain some of its former prestige and power, to the persecutory and domineering, as was the case in Paraguay. Here President Carlos Antonio López and later his grandnephew Francisco Solanos López outlawed traditional acts of reverence, such as kneeling toward the bishops, and prohibited them from using the episcopal throne or official vestments. Antonio López named his own brother archbishop of Asunción. The Lópezes cut off all communication between the Paraguayan church and Rome, isolating and turning it into a personal fiefdom. Teaching the divine right of the president became mandatory, especially as Francisco Solanos dragged the country into a suicidal war against Argentina, Brazil, and Uruguay, during which the bishops were forced into complicity by preaching obedience, holy war, and heavenly recompense for those who would give their lives for their country. The weakening of the Catholic Church continued apace as government after government forbade the payment of the tithe that traditionally supported the church and its functions and instead placed the clergy on the state payroll. The symbolism of those actions would be clear as day. Civil marriage became the law of the land, allowing even Protestant unions to be recognized. The state took control of the civil registry and education. By the early twentieth century freedom of conscience had been established throughout the continent.

Despite this, the Catholic Church nonetheless recovered some of its former strength in part thanks to a revival in pious devotions, some of which, such as the consecration of the nation to the Sacred Heart of Jesus, connected to nationalist sentiments. The fact that the church was essentially a department of the state in many countries was of benefit to the extent that the governments, especially in periods of Conservative rule, rebuilt churches, allowed foreign priests to replenish the meager clergy, opened universities and seminaries, and permitted the religious orders to return. Usually coming from France, Spain, Italy, and the United States, orders such as the Passionists, Salesians, Claretians, and Hospitallars were integral in the establishment of schools, universities, hospitals, orphanages, and homes for the elderly. Missions to isolated Indian groups recommenced, though unfortunately, as in the case of Chile and Argentina, they were sometimes used by the state as the groundwork for conquest and genocide in the interests of Europeanization and economic expansion. An effect of these policies among the rural poor, the indigenous, and the former slaves (in Brazil) was the rise of utopian and messianic movements that sought to resist secular encroachments, dissolution of traditional piety, or forced modernization.

Moreover, in the last decades of the century the Catholic Church itself began to swing in an ultramontane direction, repositioning its axis from the local bishops to the papacy, a process culminating in the Vatican I decree on papal infallibility (which was supported by all of the council's Latin American bishops). In 1858 the Latin American Pontifical College was founded in Rome, providing Latin Americans a quality and Romanized education. Even the agenda of the Latin American Plenary Council, which convened bishops from throughout the region to Rome in 1899, was dictated by Europeans set on conforming the Latin American church to a Vatican-centered model.

The status and power that the church had in the nineteenth century, even when weakened, was greatly diminished by the first third of the twentieth. In Cuba and Puerto Rico, church and state had been sundered by the power of that great theologian, the US military, and in the case of Puerto Rico the church's hierarchy, formerly Spanish, was now American. The Catholic Church in Mexico emerged limping out of a bloody revolution whose anticlerical 1917 Constitution left it virtually marginalized, officially silenced, and without property. The government would continue to see the church as an impediment to progress and sought to control and limit it, actions that culminated in the bloody Cristero War of 1926 to 1929. In Uruguay the transition to secularism, while smoother, was no less abrupt, as disestablishment even transformed the calendar's traditional holidays; Christmas became Family Day, for example.

1:4: Christianity and the End of Christendom (1930–1964)

Populist governments and a changing world order challenged the churches. Long accustomed to power, some sought to remain in the center. Others remained on the margins seeking to influence society in starkly different ways.

1:4:1: Christianity and Social Doctrine

Even as the 1864 Syllabus of Errors informed Catholic leaders of the dangers of the modern world, the church's social encyclicals, beginning with 1891's *Rerum Novarum* on capital and labor (and later *Quadragesimo Anno* in 1931), would illumine the Latin American church's path as it entered a new century. In this new era the laity would take on innovative roles. Awakened to the challenges of modernism, socialism, and the growing disparities between the rich and the poor in an increasingly industrialized society, women and men were inspired by the social doctrines of the church that sought to address these new realities. Laypeople from the middle class and lower portions of the upper class looked for ways in which society could be Christianized without necessarily returning to the days when the church dictated policy as well as conscience. They joined movements such as Catholic Action in order to influence politics and social mores. In many countries this movement served as the precursor to modern Christian Democratic parties. Hospitals, schools, and other benevolent organizations were founded, efforts that became more crucial as the region entered the Great Depression. Catholic universities multiplied, allowing intellectuals the opportunity to reflect on the role of Catholicism within their national contexts. Many social and political leaders were graduates of these institutions.

1:4:2: Piety and Practice

In this modern version of Catholicism, faith became more introspective, nurtured by popular devotion, religious knowledge, and access to the sacraments. Since education, marriage, and other aspects of the public sphere had become secularized, the church began to stress the importance of the family unit in order to transmit religious instruction, stave off the challenge of Protestantism, and influence greater society. A renewed emphasis on the Eucharist, as exemplified in the introduction of regular local and national Eucharistic congresses, fed into individual piety while also fostering a sense of the body religious that was now distinct from the body politic.

1:4:3: The "New Christendom"

The relationship between church and state in this period should be approached through the global perspective of economic insecurity, a world war, and the specter of communism. The efforts of the papacy to preserve its structures and institutions amid totalitarian and Soviet-style states throughout Europe from the 1930s to 1950s was reflected through similar anxieties in Latin America. The church had long maintained an anticommunist stance. The fear of atheistic revolutions, including Mexico's anticlerical dalliance with socialism, informed its position, as did its traditional alliance to conservative politics and traditional oligarchies. After World War II, US concerns and economic and military power dominated the hemisphere. In the midst of anticommunist, Cold War sentiment, the Catholic Church wound up making strange bedfellows with populist and often authoritarian dictators who promised protection, prosperity, and a return to traditional values. And so, in the name of security and peace, the church discovered itself waking up next to the likes of Perón (Argentina), where the church supported his rule at least in the beginning, Vargas (Brazil), Trujillo (Dominican Republic), Stroessner (Paraguay), and Somoza (Nicaragua), to name a few. This "New Christendom" of forming advantageous alliances with the powerful in government and industry was both complemented and undermined by a slowly growing faction of those who sought to move the church in a direction of social responsibility.

1:4:4: Evangelicals and Pentecostals

Evangelical missions continued apace throughout the beginning of the century. They never grew in significant numbers and so never truly posed a challenge to Catholic dominance. Their social footprint in the form of schools, hospitals, clinics, and other charitable institutions would not become significant until later in the century. Yet, they remained the perpetual other. Evangelicals placed themselves outside the traditions of many communities; they did not participate in patronal celebrations, they did not honor the Virgin, and their code of personal morality was often stricter, with an abhorrence of drinking or smoking, for example. To make matters worse, evangelicals most often sympathized with the Liberal party, especially in matters of religious liberty and the secularization of national institutions such as marriage. This placed them at odds with both the Catholic Church and the Conservatives, and it became all too easy to target them as agents of liberalism and enemies of the faith. In Colombia from 1948 to 1958, this kind of suspicion and enmity resulted in the persecution, slaughter, and dispossession of many Protestants. While it represents an extreme reaction, evangelicals throughout the continent nonetheless continued to be viewed with suspicion, originally as traitors to their (Roman Catholic) culture and later as agents or dupes of the United States as that nation took a greater role in the political, economic, and military life of the region.

Pentecostalism emerged in Latin America through various streams. It first manifested itself within the Methodist Church of Chile in 1909, predating many US denominations. In Argentina, it was introduced via European missionaries, whereas in the Caribbean and Mexico it resulted from the aftershocks of the Los Angeles Azusa Street revivals of 1906 that inspired Spirit-baptized Hispanics to return to their places of origin to spread the message. American missionaries, sometimes acting independently but most often through now-established denominations, were the first to bring Pentecostalism to Central America, Brazil, and the Andes region. The movement proved divisive and controversial to the older evangelical churches in which it emerged, its fervent believers often forced out of their churches to form their own congregations and denominations. With their exuberant worship, glossolalia, and physical manifestations of spiritual ecstasy, these early Pentecostals were often shunned, challenged, and even violently persecuted within their communities, sometimes at the instigation of local priests. During these early decades Pentecostalism spread mainly among the poor, immigrants, laborers, and the dispossessed. Though overall the movement did not experience significant growth until after the 1950s, denominations began to proliferate nonetheless. Concerns over doctrinal purity and worship, the autonomous nature of the individual congregations, and the reliance on Spirit-led charismatic leaders quickly led to factions that resulted in church-splits and the establishment of competing denominations.

Within both evangelical and Pentecostal mission churches, conflicts arose over the nature and control of these congregations. Native leadership had developed through the many schools, seminaries, and distance education programs established by foreign missionaries. However, in many cases ultimate control was retained by the missionaries and their home denominations. From the 1930s onward, a new generation of national leaders began to question this assumption. Were the churches to reflect the values and traditions of the United States or would they be permitted to develop within the contexts of their own communities and countries? What legitimate reason was there to exclude native pastors and teachers from controlling their own denominations, their institutions, and finances? These divisions, often bitter, resulted in the formation of new denominations and organizations under the control of native-born leaders. Oftentimes these acrimonious splits would not be healed for decades, and the new churches suffered from a loss of financial and infrastructural support that remained with the foreign missionaries.

Nonetheless, as these churches arose and as efforts began to cross denominational lines to form organizations for mutual support and cooperation, it marked the beginnings of a truly Latin American Protestantism.

1:5: Christianity in the Modern World (1964–present)

The last several decades of the twentieth century were a time of often-violent upheaval in Latin American society. They also marked a point of change and revolution within Christianity as old institutions reinvented themselves and new expressions of the faith came to the forefront.

1:5:1: Effects of Vatican II

The Second Vatican Council redefined the Catholic Church in the modern world. The conception of the church as the entire people of God, a reconfiguring of relationships with Protestants, Jews, and members of other religions, and the reformation of worship and piety have all been front and center in the description of the council. Furthermore, the loosening of the centripetal force tying the global church to Rome and the mandate to root the mission of the church within national and local contexts and needs allowed bishops, clergy, and religious orders to avail themselves of already percolating powers at the grassroots, pastoral, and academic levels.

Catholic Charismatic Renewal (CCR)

The charismatic movement is a global phenomenon that began in the late 1950s and early 1960s within Roman Catholicism and historic and evangelical Protestant denominations. It emphasizes experiences typically associated with Pentecostalism such as glossolalia, healing, spiritual gifts, and ecstatic worship. The movement was introduced first into Bolivia and Peru in 1970 by Father Francis MacNutt, a US priest who led teams of Catholic and Protestant leaders to hold spiritual retreats. Through their efforts, renewal spread throughout Latin America, becoming a source of revitalization within the Catholic Church at a period when the churches, fresh from Vatican II, were experimenting in novel forms of outreach, catechesis, and dialogue. In 1973 the first Latin American Catholic Charismatic Conference was held in Bogotá. The CCR has taken on a variety of forms since its inception. In Colombia, for example, the focus is on social action, whereas in Mexico it is on education and catechesis. The movement has been strongest in Brazil but now, despite early hesitation, has enjoyed the support of all the Latin American bishops' conferences both because of its role in attracting marginal or disaffected Catholics and as a counterweight to the attraction of Pentecostalism. In fact, though the growth of conservative Protestantism has drawn the lion's share of scholarly and media attention, it is estimated that at over seventy-five million adherents the CCR outnumbers self-identified Pentecostals in the region.

Liberation Theology

As populist governments began to crumble under military dictatorships beginning in the late 1950s, it became apparent to many that the "New Christendom" model was a failure. Theologians and clergy had taken their studies to Europe where an encounter with the social sciences led them to begin reflecting theologically on the situation in Latin America, beset by violence, war, underdevelopment, and a widening inequality between the wealthy and the poor. Young people in Catholic Action, priests, and members of religious orders, radicalized by their experience among the poor, began to consider the new prophetic and servant models of the church opened by the Second Vatican Council. Similarly, Protestants, mainly from the historic denominations, had been recently emancipated from missionary control and began to identify with the poor through their own ministries. The Argentine priest and scholar, Enrique Dussel, in 1967 began looking into a reappraisal of the history of the Latin American church, and the next year Presbyterian theologian Rubem Alves began to consider the role of religion in liberation. Gustavo Gutiérrez coined the term *theology of liberation* at a conference of theologians and ministers in 1968. By the time the Second General Conference of Latin American Bishops met in Medellín that year, the formation of a new type of theological reflection was in the air. Breaking with almost five centuries of habit, the bishops distanced the Latin American church from its traditional alliance with the government and the powerful and moved toward a "preferential option for the poor." Medellín addressed institutionalized violence against the poor and spoke of upturning and transforming oppressive societal structures in the name of justice. In the coming years priests, ministers, female and male religious, and laypeople from throughout the continent would reflect and elucidate on the basic question, what does it mean to be a Christian within the Latin American context? As the church sided itself with the poor, Christian base communities (CEB) became an important resource for its pastoral, liturgical, and theological life. Begun in Brazil in the late 1960s, these were small groups that met under the supervision of a priest to discuss a biblical passage and its relevance to the participants' lives. As workers, farmers, housewives, and fishers came together, they began to talk about issues such as employment, housing, medical care, and violence in light of the

Scriptures. This process of conscientization inspired people to begin taking part in voting drives, protests, and mass demonstrations against repressive governments throughout the next several decades.

Liberation theology came under critique from traditionalist religious leaders both for its use of Marxist class analysis and for its confrontational or unaccommodating nature vis-à-vis national governments and wealthy oligarchies. This alarm was especially acute given the events of the Cuban Revolution and the repression of the church in communist Cuba. Pope John Paul II, with John Ratzinger as prefect of the Congregation for the Doctrine of the Faith, was especially antagonistic toward it, believing that liberationists sought to replace the kingdom of God with a human-made utopia brought about by class warfare. Under his papacy, left-leaning bishops were transferred or, when retired, replaced with traditionalist prelates, often from the controversial conservative group Opus Dei. In 1985 the Vatican would silence Brazilian theologian Leonardo Boff for a year and a decade later silenced Ivone Gebara for a period of two years. Despite these challenges, many of Medellín's priorities were reiterated at CELAM's 1979 conference in Puebla, Mexico. As violence, assassination, and guerrilla warfare increased throughout Latin America in the 1970s and 1980s, the stakes and the risks associated with speaking out on behalf of human dignity became ever higher.

1:5:2: Churches under Dictatorships

The repressive military dictatorships that ruled throughout most of Latin America from the 1970s to the early 1990s must be seen within the context of the Cold War. The United States had a long history of supporting right-wing governments, first out of economic concern to American businesses and then in an effort to stem communist influence on the continent. Left-wing militias had begun to emerge in the 1960s and 1970s, often supported by the Soviet Union and Cuba. Practically the entire region was engaged in a proxy war on behalf of the two great superpowers. In the middle were the masses of people, mainly the poor, whom neither the governments nor the militias represented. Throughout this period those who actively opposed the government, who protested, sought to register voters, or participated in any activity that the state considered subversive or sympathetic to communism paid the price. Many were "disappeared," raped, tortured, mutilated, murdered; entire villages were obliterated if suspected by one side of aiding the other. Beginning in the 1960s, parts of the Catholic Church had begun to break with the age-old tradition of supporting the "God-ordained" secular powers. Priests, nuns, friars, theologians, laypeople, and bishops in many parts of the region began to speak and act out against the violence. For many who suffered or whose family members had been taken in the night, the church became the only place that would listen to their pleas, recording their testimonies and, when possible, providing information, news, asylum, legal aid, and other resources to those in need. Where the church took an active role in opposing the repression, Catholic universities were subject to government control, churches, homes, and other religious buildings were vandalized, the bishops were spied upon, and clerics and ministers were arrested, tortured, threatened, and murdered. Yet the witness of these Christians remained strong. During Argentina's Dirty War and beyond, the Mothers of the Plaza de Mayo silently marched in protest every week to demand news of their disappeared relatives. In Pinochet's Chile, Cardinal Raul Silva Henríquez organized support efforts. The archbishop of Guatemala, Próspero Penados del Barrio, openly denounced that government's violence. Cardinal Paulo Evaristo Arns and Presbyterian Jaime Wright joined forces to document Brazil's human rights abuses. Bishop Juan José Gerardi Conedera did the same in Guatemala and the day after publishing his findings was murdered in his garage by soldiers. More controversially, Camilo Torres, a Colombian priest, laid aside his clerical collar in 1965 to join the guerrillas against the government. In El Salvador the 1980s began with the rape and murder of three missionary nuns and a lay worker, and it ended with the assassination of six Jesuit teachers, their housekeeper, and her daughter. Of course, one has to mention the untiring efforts for peace, human dignity, and reconciliation on the part of Archbishop Oscar Romero, whose blood was mingled with that of the consecrated wine when he was shot while officiating at Mass.

This is not to say that the light shone in the darkness everywhere. Argentina's episcopate remained largely silent and possibly collaborated with the government throughout that country's Dirty War. In Guatemala, Archbishop Mario Casariego was supportive of military rule and dismissed reports of human rights abuses and murdered priests, even as he blessed the army's tanks with holy water.

The record for the Protestant churches is more ambiguous. Resistance to the dictatorships came primarily from the historic, mainline traditions with a history of biblical and theological criticism. However, that is not to say that more conservative factions did not exist within those groups. Rubem Alves was denounced as a subversive by his own Presbyterian Church, and members of the Lutheran Church in Chile called on the Pinochet government to exile Helmut Frenz for his actions on behalf of human rights. Evangelicals and Pentecostals tended to preserve traditions of quietism or support toward government authorities as well as strong anticommunist sentiment, sometimes informed by larger religious and political concerns. The situation in Guatemala under the short presidency of Efraín Ríos Montt points to the connections between the Religious Right in the United States and the American presidency. Ministers such as televangelist Pat Robertson perceived the struggle against godless communism in apocalyptic terms. Meanwhile, the Reagan administration suspected liberation theology of being a form of Soviet infestation and indoctrination. The concerns of these intertwined groups came together in Montt, a Pentecostal who wanted to return Christian family values to the country and an avowed enemy of communism. Under him, Roman Catholic priests and catechists were targeted by the military as Communist sympathizers for their efforts to help the rural Maya. Conservative Pentecostals and evangelicals, often with institutional and financial ties to their US brethren and who could enjoy programs like *The 700 Club* where their president was heralded as a hero of the faith, tended to support the Montt government and even benefited from its distribution of food and resources. The situation was not unique to Guatemala. A year after Pinochet took power, the Catholic Church refused to celebrate the traditional Te Deum service in his honor. The Methodist Pentecostal Church quickly assumed the task, and twenty-five hundred evangelical ministers signed a document declaring their loyalty to the dictator.

In 1979 the Sandinistas entered Managua, Nicaragua, in victory. They were supported by several Roman Catholic clerics, including Ernesto Cardenal, who took positions in the new government. Pope John Paul II ordered the priests to resign. Their refusal culminated in a very public rebuke of Cardenal on the airport tarmac during the pope's 1983 visit. When the crowds later clamored their desire for peace, the pontiff's "¡Silencio!" seemed indicative of his impatience with the entire movement. A long decade of battle against the US-funded contras, the opposition of the bishops, and the disappointing, unfulfilled promise of the Sandinistas ended with that government's demise in 1990. A generation's dreams of creating a better world order seemed to vanish into mist. Yet, free elections were finally held. Across the Americas, military governments toppled and democracies were restored, with the Catholic Church often serving as a mediator for peace and reconciliation. By the middle of the decade, the Soviet Union and the fear of a continental communist takeover were gone. Christianity in Latin America would once again be faced with the challenges of a new world order.

1:5:3: Christianity under New Democracies

The restoration of democracy throughout Latin America ignited the hope that the will of the people would be reflected in their governments. In the absence of the military, political, and economic threat of the Soviet Union, however, neoliberalism, dominated by the economic power of the United States, was able to exercise virtual hegemony over the region. History repeated itself in Latin America as powerful oligarchies, composed of the upper and middle classes, traded in one political system for another and took advantage of the new state of affairs. As a result, the masses of the poor, of Indians, and of other minorities were blocked from the possibility of development and of having their voices heard. Poverty, violence, need, and exploitation, along with drug abuse, prostitution, gangs, and environmental crises, have been the fallout of the new world order.

The Church as Moral Compass

After the horrors of the previous decades, the Catholic Church in general emerged stronger. In many countries it had distinguished itself through martyrdom. Having been the voice of conscience and human dignity to many, it has continued to serve as one of the most respected institutions of the region, especially in areas where bishops, priests, and religious identify with the everyday struggles of the people. In many countries where the movement to secularism continues through restrictions on the church's power or through policies that take into account the present multicultural, multireligious, modern world, Catholics, Protestants, and a small smattering of Orthodox seek to present a common Christian moral, ethical, and sacramental worldview. The churches have spoken out against economic inequality, government corruption, and racial and ethnic discrimination and have served as mediators between governments, labor unions, street gangs, and militias. Even hard-line Cuba has softened its attitude on religious observance in the last decade. In recent years Christians have also taken to the streets against a relaxation of restrictions on abortion and proposals for same-sex marriage. Reflecting the diversity that exists within Christianity, however, some religious leaders and denominations have also expressed support on behalf of the rights of religious minorities (such as practitioners of Santería), of women, and for lesbians and gays.

Liberation 2.0

After the Soviet demise, many observers believed that liberation theology would silently disappear, basing their assessment on the belief that it depended exclusively on Marxism. Yet, as others have pointed out, Marxist class analysis was simply a tool through which to analyze the social inequalities present on the continent (and regardless, even if Soviet-style communism was a thing of the past, its fall did not discredit the analysis itself). Nonetheless, the failure of the Nicaraguan experiment appeared to serve as a humbling experience, reminding people that the neither the just society nor the eschatological hope would be built through human hands. While the active involvement of church leaders and theologians in partisan politics did ebb significantly, the critique of politics, economics, and social relations from the preferential option for the poor has only increased. A new generation of men and women has given voice to the multiple oppressions present in modern society. *Mujerista* theology addresses machismo and gender disparities. Caribbean theology, in various forms, begins with the distinct social and economic realities of that region. Afro-Latin, gay, and indigenous people, among others, offer an assessment of systemic discrimination and violence. In the United States, long-marginalized Hispanic groups, socially conscious since the 1960s, have developed Latino, Chicano, Nuyorican, Cuban-American, and other theological and pastoral expressions pertinent to their particular experiences. Using sources such as the Bible, tradition, popular piety, music, myth, midrash, gender and queer studies, and other tools, they propose perspectives and critiques in the hope of presenting a fuller vision of Christian truth toward understanding and reconciliation between peoples.

Pentecostals and Power

One of the most talked about developments in recent decades has been the visible and astounding growth of evangelical, particularly Pentecostal, churches throughout Latin America. These churches can be categorized as historic Pentecostal denominations connected with early Pentecostal growth or missionary efforts (such as those of the Assemblies of God or the Church of the Foursquare Gospel), independent denominations that arose in the middle of the century under native leadership, and the neo-Pentecostal/charismatic churches that are more recent, usually disconnected from older traditions, and sometimes associated with popular megachurches and movements. The growth of these traditions has been variously attributed to US imperialism, the attraction of grassroots leadership, the formation of communities in dehumanizing urban centers, and the promise of miraculous healing for those who cannot afford doctors. Another reason might be Pentecostalism's commonalities with traditional Latin American spirituality that dates back to the baroque period (as well as African and indigenous religion). For both Pentecostalism and popular religion, the divine is immanent and palpable through ritual and emotion; whereas in popular Catholicism the divine might be found at a local shrine, for Pentecostals it would be at a revival meeting. Both belief systems posit the entry of the supernatural into everyday lives through divine healing and sacred objects (a relic or saint's statue for the one, anointing oil or the Bible for the other). And both are forms of mass religiosity not defined by institutional structures (though may be complemented by them). Catholic folk piety is accessible to all, standing outside church control, as in a private home altar or popular religious site. In Pentecostalism, the Spirit is given extravagantly to all who seek it, and leadership is traditionally determined by the presence of charismatic gifts rather than institutional credentials. Some have pointed to the wild success of this tradition in Brazil, a region where spiritism has taken root and African-derived beliefs about the immanence of the supernatural world are prevalent. In short, I argue that Pentecostalism, rather than the historic Protestant traditions, has taken hold of the continent precisely because the former is the flip side of Latin American popular religion (whether defined as baroque, Catholic, Afro-Latin, and so on).

Because Pentecostalism is defined by spiritual experience, some churches have taken on heterodox beliefs and practices, such as distinguishing modes of dress, millennial visions, or the prophetic or semidivine role of the church's founder. For example, the current leader of the Light of the World, Samuel Joaquín Flores, is regarded as God's apostle on earth, and the Samaria Evangelical Church of Puerto Rico is Sabbatarian and requires women to wear head coverings during worship. Separation from surrounding society, either literally through physical communities or through modes of behavior and dress, serves as an identity marker that also distinguishes believers from unbelievers, reinforcing members' belief in themselves as the elect, the sanctified, and the like.

The new generation of Pentecostal churches has not been without controversy, though. Aside from the alarm that some Roman Catholic church leaders, including Benedict XVI, have expressed at the growth of the "sects," accusations of financial mismanagement, religious intolerance, and cultlike behavior have followed some. The lack of institutional oversight and the centrality of gifted, charismatic leaders make such churches vulnerable to issues of power and control held in the name of God. In recent years there have been allegations of sexual abuse and financial mismanagement against Light of the World's pastor in Mexico. The leaders of Brazil's Reborn in Christ Church have recently been embroiled in a number of investigations connected to accusations of money laundering, tax evasion, forgery, and embezzlement. Even distinctive theological beliefs serve as sources of controversy. Guatemala's El Shaddai teaches a materialistic prosperity gospel that some view as an exploitation of the poor, while ministers of Brazil's Universal Church of the Kingdom of God infamously kicked over a statue of the nation's patron saint during a televised service. Their attacks on Catholicism, Afro-Brazilian religions, Islam, Judaism, and even other Protestant churches have been provocative to say the least.

Pentecostal traditions in Latin America tend to be theologically, ethically, and politically conservative. Many of them have been informed by US dispensational evangelicalism and often reflect a pro–United States, pro-Israel perspective. However, unlike many

Pentecostal traditions in the United States that have traditionally focused on missions and evangelism to the exclusion of social justice, many Pentecostal denominations in Latin America, including the megachurches, have also been involved in establishing schools, clinics, employment and counseling services, and other social works. In some regions, such as Brazil and Central America, Pentecostalism is often seen as a path toward middle-class respectability and an escape from violence, emphasizing family ties and personal morality, including an honest work ethic and abstention from alcohol and drugs. However, that individual empowerment for some has also translated into political activism. Coming from the poor and middle classes, some have successfully run for local, regional, and nationwide office to represent their communities. Pentecostals from the favelas in Brazil have lobbied politicians for improvements in living conditions and infrastructure; their numbers and influence guarantee that politicians who ignore this demographic might not fare so well at the next elections. The pattern has been repeated elsewhere; the president of Guatemala and other government dignitaries attended the 2007 dedication of the Christian Fraternity of Guatemala's new temple, a sign of the growing importance of that country's Pentecostal community.

North of the Border

The earliest explorers into what would become the United States were Spanish soldiers and friars who crossed no borders, seeking wealth as they explored northward from New Spain and across the Caribbean into Florida and the Gulf and Eastern seaboards. Franciscan and Jesuit missionaries sought out converts as they trekked through the American Southwest, most famously Junípero Serra who established California's famous missions. The story of the evangelization of the native peoples in this region remained one of tragedy. Gathered into *reducciones* by force and made to work for the Spanish settlements, they were gradually stripped of their culture and religion. The ensuing Pueblo Revolt of 1680 was the only successful Indian rebellion against a colonial power, even if its success was short-lived.

The Hispanic presence in the United States has often been described not only as the crossing of people over the border, but as the border crossing over people. Instances of the latter were the results of the Mexican War of 1846-1848 when the United States took over what amounted to half of Mexico's territory and the acquisition of Puerto Rico in the 1898 war against Spain. Whereas Puerto Ricans were granted US citizenship in 1917 and could now freely move across the mainland, other groups have arrived mainly as the result of economic necessity (Mexicans), as exiles (Cubans), or as refugees displaced by armed conflict and violence (Central Americans). Usually settling in larger urban centers, they have succeeded in forming vibrant communities despite the challenges of marginalization, prejudice, and disenfranchisement. As for many immigrant groups, religion has served as a wellspring of identity and resilience. However, this was not always easy. When Mexicans across California and the Southwest awoke in the mid-nineteenth century to find themselves citizens of a new country, they also discovered that they now belonged to a Roman Catholic Church governed primarily by Irish and German prelates who held little sympathy for their traditions and spirituality. Disputes between church leaders and laypersons ensued, often driving the people away from the institutional church and further into the world of folk piety.

The church was slow to respond to the spiritual needs of Mexicans and other Hispanics. Though Spanish-language chapels were established in cities, the drive towards change within the Catholic

Church has not come from above but from below, from among the people and their priests. The Chicano movement of the 1960s, calling for the rights and recognition of Mexican-Americans, drew on the spiritual roots of the people even as the civil rights movement in African-American communities relied on the power of the black church. The Virgin of Guadalupe accompanied striking laborers organized by civil rights leaders, César Chávez, himself a fervent Catholic, and Dolores Huerta. This sense of ethnic and cultural pride itself became reflected back into the religious sphere as people of Latin American descent, men and women, lay and clerical, Catholic and Protestant, have asserted the value and dignity of their spiritual traditions and have embarked on the task of doing theology from the perspectives of the multifaceted Latino/a experience.

Puerto Ricans, Cubans, South Americans and others arriving in the US often encounter a larger spiritual marketplace that offers a plethora of Protestant and non-Christian religious alternatives. Evangelical and Pentecostal traditions, characterized by emotional worship, a stress on the immanence of the divine, and grassroots leadership have especially appealed to and benefitted from the Hispanic presence. The relative ease of movement and communication between countries that enable Latinos to maintain ties with their countries of origin have allowed for a cultural and religious cross-fertilization to occur between US Hispanic groups and their compatriots across the hemisphere, in the process revitalizing Christian expressions of faith everywhere. In consequence, the Hispanic demographic has spurred changes and adaptations in liturgy, language, music, education, and theology across the denominational lines.

Second and third generation Hispanics bring with them a greater sense of belonging and not belonging; of having roots in Latin America while having feet firmly planted in the United States. More assimilated than their parents, their presence in multiracial, English-speaking congregations becomes an opportunity to practice the Latin American experience of *mestizaje* as cultural outlooks, traditions, and spiritualities are adapted and re-created to and fro. The Latina/o demographic in the United States shows no sign of abatement, ensuring for many (in hope or in fear) that by mid-century, the country may well be considered a part of Latin America itself, yet with its own distinctive voices.

Challenges and Opportunities

As Latin American Christianity moves further into the twenty-first century, its role within modern society is all but certain. The religious diversity of the region has become apparent to all. A small Eastern Orthodox presence, not only among Middle Eastern and Russian immigrants but also among Maya communities in Guatemala and elsewhere, has begun to join in dialogue with their Catholic and Protestant coreligionists. Popular religious movements not only reflect official and unofficial Catholic piety but now include Santa Muerte, UFOlogy, New Age beliefs, and others contending for spiritual allegiance throughout all social classes. Indigenous groups, professing both traditional religions and Christianity, have made their presence and just demand for equal rights known. Historically overlooked Afro-Latin communities have also raised their voices. In the past, traditions such as Candomblé and Umbanda have had to be practiced underground, but they are now becoming points of national pride in some areas and are afforded equal legal protections.

The Roman Catholic Church itself is a diverse and sometimes divided body. Traditionalist bishops, many appointed by Pope John Paul II, dominate the hierarchy and sometimes reflect the wish to return to the age of church-state alliances. Meanwhile, charismatic renewal continues to revitalize the spiritual and evangelistic life of much of the laity, and a steady current of liberationism, often at odds with the conservatism of the hierarchy as well as the last two popes, seeks the radical transformation of society's values and structures. Though at times it appears that the Catholic Church is seeking to replicate the model of the "New Christendom," the diverse streams within the church serve as a system of checks and balances that do not permit any one model of the church to dominate throughout society. What voices will come to steer Catholicism as the current generation ages? Within Protestantism, there are divisions between theological and social conservatives and progressives, who often confess liberationist convictions and support for women's equality and gay rights. In recent years, several nations have taken on typically secularist policies as regards religious pluralism, sex education, women's reproductive rights, and homosexuality. The challenge of reaching a progressively secularizing yet paradoxically religious population is but one of Christianity's challenges and opportunities.

The problems of the continent are endemic: cartel-related violence in Mexico, the abuse and murder of homeless children in Brazil, widespread street gangs in El Salvador, the exploitation of the Amazon, and wealth that remains concentrated in the hands of the powerful who have benefited from neoliberal economic reforms and that push thousands to risk their lives northward towards the United States are only a few that make the headlines. The election of Jorge Bergoglio in 2013 to lead the world's 1.2 billion Roman Catholics has brought renewed attention to the continent, its contributions to the larger Christian world, and the immeasurable resource that is its people's faith in the midst of unimaginable adversity.

2

Brief Introduction to Theology in Latin America

2:1: Introduction

The task of summarizing a theological enterprise that covers a continent, five centuries, and the many fields of theology from the role of the saints to Christology to the very nature of God would either be an act of insanity or hubris of Greek proportions.[1] Overall, Latin American theology, particularly in the period before 1960, is little known outside of narrow academic circles. Most descriptions in popular or college texts begin with Bartolomé de Las Casas (1484–1566) and then jump to the formation of liberation theology

---

1. The best effort to do so is currently the three-volume, 3,500-page work edited by Josep-Ignaci Saranyana. Comprehensive and using not only official or academic theological sources but also sermons, catechisms, and popular periodicals, *Teología en América Latina* (Madrid: Iberoamericana, 1999–2002) is only available in Spanish and found in a smattering of university libraries. Saranyana's shorter and far lighter summarization, *Breve historia de la teología en América Latina* (Madrid: Biblioteca de Autores Cristianos, 2009), begs for an English-language translation.

in the modern era. In fact, the phrase "Latin American theology" is often used as a synonym for that latter school of thought.

For the purposes of this introduction, I propose a manageable scheme that takes into account one of the major questions posed during the three main periods of Latin American Christianity. For the colonial period, there is the issue of anthropology. As Christians first began to encounter the American continent, questions arose: Who are they? Are they rational human beings? What is our responsibility toward them? As the colonial enterprise ventured forth, the relationship between the Christian faith and native traditions began to be addressed. Finally, at the close of the period, when Creoles began to look at the role of the Americas within salvation history, the question became, who are we?

The independence movements of the early nineteenth century ruptured the assumed alliance of church and Crown. As the church teetered between unstable Liberal and Conservative republics, the question of the day turned to matters of church and society: What is the proper relationship between the City of God and the City of Man? How can we create a Christian society in the modern world? Protestants, mostly from the United States, entered the stage with their own assumptions about the individual and society, salvation, and freedom.

As the "New Christendom" model began to break down in the face of repressive military dictatorships, a new awareness of the continent's socioeconomic problems galvanized a generation of leaders who were energized by Vatican II and whose work was facilitated by modern means of communication and communion. While at one point it seemed enough to demand doctrinal and moral adherence and submission to the church to guarantee salvation, liberation theology's one-eighty on what it means to be a Christian in the midst of poverty and violence raised soteriological questions:

What does Christianity consist of? What is sin? What does salvation, now and in the *eschaton*, look like? As surely as radicalized Catholics and Protestants offered one perspective, conservative Pentecostalism, empowered by the Spirit, began to pose an alternative.

2:1:1: Foundations

The formation of theology in Latin America is rooted in the European patristic and medieval traditions. Though it is developed in response to the particular questions and needs of the Latin American context, looking into the basic presuppositions of the region's theological tradition regarding society and knowledge is necessary.

Augustine's Legacy

It has been said that the whole of Western theology is but a footnote to Augustine of Hippo (354-430). Catholic and Protestant thinking, essentially the flip sides of the same coin, follow or react to the African bishop's reflections on God, human nature, grace, salvation, the church, and sacraments. In the *City of God*, written in response to the sack of Rome in 410, Augustine posits the Heavenly City, the now-and-not-yet commonwealth made up of the redeemed and guided by the love of God, in contrast to the Earthly City, led by the love of self. The church is made up of people from both worlds, their identities and allegiances unknown until the fulfillment of time. In the Middle Ages, this idea was tweaked to form Christendom, the community that, with the pope as its head, exists to bring sin-born people into the City of God. Christianity, in this way, became coterminous with civilization. A symbiotic relationship was expected to exist between the church and the state whereby Christian rulers were to facilitate and support the church in its mission of preaching the gospel, extending its presence, and administering the sacraments. The church, in return, was assumed to bless the state in its economic, political, and military endeavors. Baptism was the entryway not only into the sacramental life of the church but also into Christian society. This was the way of life both at the beginning of Iberian colonization and throughout Latin America until the various republics began the process of disestablishment in the mid-nineteenth century.

Scholasticism

Scholasticism, often associated with the High Middle Ages, can be summarized as the exploration between reason and faith. How far can human reason take us toward Christian truth? How are the doctrines of Christianity better grasped through reflection and logic? By the end of the Middle Ages, one of the dominant forms of Scholasticism became one understood through the writings of Aristotle, rediscovered in the West in the thirteenth century. Here, reason was perceived as a universal given, divorced from cultural assumptions. The result was that the beliefs, worldviews, experiences, and practices of a given people were considered secondary at best and idolatrous at worst, to be extirpated. Thus Christianity, as spread throughout the New World, was presented as a matter of rational assent followed by a change in behavior rather than as experience, relationship, or acculturation.

2:2: Colonial Period: "Are They Not Men?"

The Spanish "discovery" of the inhabitants of the New World was earth-shattering. The existence of a new continent tore at the geographical conception of the continents—Europe, Africa, and Asia reflecting the perfect number of the Trinity. The table of nations in Genesis 10 did not account for these newly encountered people. On chancing upon the Taíno in 1492, Christopher Columbus described them as "with fine shapes and faces" and "handsomely formed." Quickly though, he recognized their economic and religious potential: "the people are ingenious, and would be good servants and I am of opinion that they would very readily become Christians, as they appear to have no religion." These two motivations repeatedly clashed throughout this early period. Religious orders sought to convert individuals through Baptism, catechesis, the destruction of idols, instilling the Commandments, and so forth. However, Spanish imperial theology—that vision, developed throughout centuries of the Reconquista, of Spain as holder of a unique place in salvation history to promulgate the gospel and rid the world of false religion through expansionist power—ran roughshod over the efforts of the friars to the extent that the mission of the church and that of the Crown became seen as one and the same by many religious. Following up on the papal distribution of the world between the Spanish and Portuguese in *Inter caetera*, the Spanish created the Requerimiento in 1513 as a way to legally and morally justify (even if dubiously to some contemporaries) the wars of conquest. In reading aloud a summary of salvation history and the demand that the natives submit to the claims of the papacy and Spanish monarchs, the case for just war was made. Even though the document was often read aloud only in Spanish, and sometimes to an empty beach or from the deck of the ship, resulting military action and the enslavement of the natives was perceived as legally and morally just.

Already in 1511 the Dominicans on the island of Hispaniola had sided with the Indians. Through their spokesperson, Antonio de Montesinos (1475–1540), they demanded of the assembled settlers that momentous Advent morning, "Are they not men? Do they not have rational souls? Are you not bound to love them as you love yourselves?" On the basis of a common humanity and the Christian ethical imperative, the Dominicans' protest threatened to subvert the economic reason for the conquest.

2:2:1: Clash of the Titans

During the first half century after the Columbian encounter, the rationality of the Indians—that is, their humanity—was constantly under question by conquerors, jurists, and theologians. The Spanish historian Gonzalo Fernández de Oviedo described them as "naturally lazy and vicious," "idolatrous, libidinous." Others described them in more bestial terms. In writing on the fierceness of the Caribs, the antithesis of the gentle Taínos, Columbus mentioned the practice of cannibalism. Queen Isabel, who had declared the natives to be free vassals under her protection, made an exception for those taking part in that disputable custom. Among conquistadors, the accusation of cannibalism quickly became a blank check by which to justify the conquest and enslavement of any people they encountered. It grew into a trait added onto the lists of detractors to prove the inhumanity of the Indians. Despite the declaration of Pope Paul III in the encyclical *Sublimus Dei* (1537) that the "Indians are truly men" and "by no means to be deprived of their liberty," the debates on the nature of the indigenous peoples continued, culminating in the Valladolid Debate of 1550–1551 between the theologian Juan Gínes de Sepúlveda (1489–1573) and the Defender of the Indians, Bartolomé de Las Casas.

Las Casas had arrived on Hispaniola in 1502 as a young man and was ordained there several years later. He was witness to the conquest of Cuba, its violence and atrocities inflicted on the natives affecting him deeply. Though given an *encomienda* of Indians, he gave it up in 1514 after a crisis of conscience led him to dedicate his life to advocating for the lives and rights of the natives before the colonists, the church, and the Spanish court. His efforts helped shape the papal pronouncements of *Sublimus Dei* and influenced the passage of the New Laws of 1542 to end the *encomienda* system. In an act unparalleled in European history, Charles I called to a halt the conquest of the Americas until the justice of Spain's military expansion could be further investigated.

Though the proceedings of the Valladolid Debate have been lost, it is not difficult to reconstruct the participants' arguments from their writings. Sepúlveda, siding with the colonists, drew on an Aristotelian understanding of humanity to justify the continued war against the Amerindians. Here, fully human beings possess *humanitas*, the capacity for morality and reason that allows them to create civilizations. Only those possessing such characteristics are deservedly free. Basing his perspective on descriptions of the Indians (of whom he had no firsthand experience), Sepúlveda declared that their barbarity, lack of morality, and idolatry made them less than human, lacking true humanity. As beings given to their baser instincts, they belong in another class of people—those who by nature are designed to be dominated by the civilized. Lacking rationality, morality, or civilization, they are fit only for slavery. Sepúlveda further argued that their conquest by the Spanish served as a positive good, preventing the practice of cannibalism or human sacrifice and placing them in a position to receive Christianity. Though by the late 1540s when he wrote his treatise *Democrates Secundus*, Sepúlveda had, in light of the papal pronouncement from the previous decade, softened some of the language regarding the necessity of force in the conquest of the Indians, his thesis regarding the enslavement and implied political usurpation of the Indians belies the changed perspective.

Las Casas drew upon his personal experiences among the natives, as witness to the wars of conquest, as well as his own biblical, humanist, and scholastic training. He began with an exhausting word-for-word reading of his own five-hundred-page Latin rebuttal of Sepúlveda's claims. In order to answer Sepúlveda's assertions on the inferiority of the Indians, Las Casas relied heavily on his *Apologetic History*, describing the history and civilizations of the Indians and pointing out how they not only fulfilled Aristotle's conditions for full humanity but were in several respects superior to the ancient Greeks and Romans. He does not discount Aristotle's categories of humanity but simply asserts that, by virtue of their culture, rationality, morality, and civilization, the Indians are not inferior beings. In answering the charge that human sacrifice proved the barbarity of the natives, he played an exaggerated game of philosophical gymnastics to remove culpability from the Indians. Admitting that they were probably in error, he nonetheless pointed out that in sacrificing fellow human beings, the indigenous truly understood the nature of sacrifice as demanding the best that one could offer. Cue the eye rolling. While repudiating the conquest of the Americas by means of violence, Las Casas had to step gingerly so as not to attack the rights of the Spanish Crown to colonize the continent. Not only did his work risk treason but also a denial of papal authority, given that the rights of expansion and evangelization had been recognized by the very bull whose pronouncements on the Indians he sought to defend. Here, the Dominican friar placed the emphasis on Spain's mission to spread the gospel, repeating, as he had done masterfully in his 1537 treatise *The Only Way*, that the only legitimate means of evangelization was peaceful, appealing to reason and acting in love. As Christ, the apostles, and their followers had gone forth to spread the good news without the use of arms, so should the Spanish.

Though both Sepúlveda and Las Casas claimed victory after Valladolid, the decisions of the judges have been lost to history. Sepúlveda was unable to publish his works afterward, perhaps due to his opponent's efforts. Las Casas, perceiving that not much at all had changed in the Americas, continued to pen, publish, prod, plead, and petition. The active enslavement of the Indians eventually ceased, in part due to new legislation and in greater part due to their extermination and the importation of African slaves. In the broader arguments regarding war, conquest, and the rights and responsibilities of combatants, the views of the Dominican theologian Francisco de Vitoria—who proposed a universal standard of conduct based on the "law of nations," the foundation of international law—would prevail.

On the ground, the perception of the Amerindians varied. At best, they were seen as children who lacked the necessary capacities to self-govern or become equal members of the church. This paternalistic and sometimes hostile framework at various times denied them the sacraments, education, or ordination (though it is a matter of record that Indians would often take advantage of this second-class citizenship to successfully sue in court for the amelioration of certain taxes or fees charged to the general population. Inferior indeed!). At its worst, the concept of the Indian as barbaric, backward, or barely human continued to be used to justify their conquest, enslavement, and even genocide even into the nineteenth and twentieth centuries. More recently, such attitudes continue to be the rationale for denying them civil rights and justice before the law, and to hand their traditional lands to loggers, oil drillers, and mining companies.[2]

---

2. The former President of Peru Alan García Pérez (2006–2011), a supporter of transnational companies seeking drilling and mining rights in the Amazon, described the indigenous worldviews as "pantheistic, absurd ideologies" that must give way in order to develop the disputed regions ("Alan Garcia contra las ideologias absurdas panteistas," posted by Jesus Manuel Sairitupac Vasquez, June 17, 2011, https://www.youtube.com/watch?v=2Vf4WfS5t08).

2:2:2: On Culture

Intimately connected with the questions surrounding the humanity of the natives were those touching on their cultures and, in particular, their religious practices. By the sixteenth century Iberian Christianity reflected an intolerance toward other religions that it had accrued since the 1200s when economic crisis and a fear of Jewish individuals in positions of power led to greater restrictions on Jews and a new, concentrated effort to convert them. Those Jews and Muslims who did convert, the so-called New Christians, were seen as tainted and potentially disingenuous. The Inquisition, controlled by the Crown, was established in 1478 to root out insincere converts who continued to practice their traditional faiths underground. This aggressive impulse to seek out and destroy competing religions followed the Catholic Church to the New World. Totems, Mayan and Aztec codices, Inca *mallquis* (mummified ancestors), and other religious artifacts were destroyed by the missionaries in their fervor to convert the Indians. In the dichotomous world of Iberian Christianity, traditional religions were perceived to be superstitious, idolatrous, and satanic.

Nonetheless, there is a stream within the faith that honored pre-Christian religions as precursors to Christianity, their symbols and practices often interpreted as types or anticipations of the gospel. The

On June 5, 2009, he ordered the Peruvian police and military to stop Amazonian protesters and their supporters from blocking loggers, miners, and oil drillers from entering the Bagua region. One hundred natives and fourteen police officers were killed in the melee. The next day, García described the indigenous as acting "savagely, barbarically, and with ferocity." A propagandist video released by the government days later, accompanied by images of spear-wielding natives, repeated the charge, adding that the "humble" and "unarmed" police officers had been assassinated by the Indians ("Spot contra el paro amozónico," posted by Lamula.pe, June 8, 2009, https://www.youtube.com/watch?v=hxUJdGipiJ4). Cf. Oscar Espinosa de Rivero. "¿Salvajes opuestos al progreso?: Aproximaciones históricas y antropológicas a las movilizaciones indígenas en la Amazonía peruana," *Antropologica* 27, no. 27 (2009): 123–68, available through Scielo Peru, http://www.scielo.org.pe/scielo.php?pid=S0254-92122009000100007&script=sci_arttext.

second-century apologist Justin Martyr believed that just as Judaism prepared the way for Christianity among the Jews, so Greco-Roman religion served as a precursor for the gentiles. Thus as the church spread throughout Europe, missionaries looked for points of contact between traditional religions and Christianity. The same occurred in the Americas as members of religious orders saw parallels between indigenous religions and Christian practices; the symbol of the cross and the ritual use of water for cleansing are two examples. However, for the missionaries, whatever innate sense of true religion that the Indians may have had was ruined by idolatry and the devil and had to be destroyed. There were a few, missionaries, Europeans, or Americans, however, who refused to accept that interpretation.

Felipe Guaman Poma de Ayala (1550–1616) was descended from Inca nobility and wrote *The First New Chronicle and Good Government* as a critique of colonial government to be presented to Philip III in the hope that the king would redress the abuses inflicted on his subjects. As a Christian Inca, Guaman Poma does not argue against the legitimacy of the conquest but rather presents the king with evidence of corruption, violence, and injustice perpetrated by both the viceregal rulers and the church. However, when it comes to indigenous history and religion, he decidedly places them within the framework of biblical and universal salvation history.

Addressing the question of Indian origins and their apparent absence in the biblical record, he asserts that Indians descended from the sons of Noah, children not of Adam's disobedience but of the universal covenant. They thus retained vestiges of true religion but fell into idolatry when they began to gather into settlements and grew covetous of gold and silver. Until the Inca introduced the worship of idols, the Indians practiced works of mercy and observed the Decalogue. This account serves not only to provide a biblical basis for indigenous origins and religion but also effectively places them on an equal footing with the Spanish; by becoming idolaters for the love of wealth, the Inca serve as a precautionary tale to the Europeans whose experience and power they prefigured.

Guaman Poma proposes that the Spanish king send a visitor-general to ameliorate the cruelties of the colonial government and reinstall the Inca rulers to govern in the Crown's name. Going further, he suggests that the pope deputize a second-in-command to administer the American church. This individual would have the effect of making Lima, the City of Kings, the nexus uniting the empires of Europe and America, an American Rome as surely as Constantinople was heir to the first. In proposing that the king replace the Spanish with Inca royalty and the pope appoint a vicar and permit the ordination of native priests, then forbidden, Guaman Poma advances the inherent dignity of indigenous rule and religiosity.

A contemporary of Guaman Poma, Blas Valera (1545–1597) was a mestizo and member of the Society of Jesus whose facility with Quechua and other indigenous languages made him invaluable in the preparation of resources through which to reach the Peruvian Indians with Christianity.[3] He was extremely interested in the preconquest cultures of the region and sought out witnesses and historical documents to aid his writing of an Inca history. Most of his works are no longer extant, though portions of them are quoted by other writers such as Garcilaso de la Vega. The *Account of the Ancient Customs of the Natives of Peru*, however, is usually attributed to him. Throughout his writings, Valera seeks to present Inca religion as an anticipation of Christianity. Drawing on the religious categories of the second-century Roman writer Marcus Terentius Varro and

3. There is a current debate, based on discovered manuscripts whose authenticity has not yet been demonstrated, that Blas Valera and Guaman Poma de Ayala are the same individual. Since that hypothesis remains unproven, for our purposes we will continue to think of them as separate persons.

Augustine of Hippo's use of him, Valera rejects the anthropomorphic and bestial deities of Mesoamerica, instead choosing to laud the Inca for their "natural religion"—that is, their worship of the sun and the planets. He pays special attention to Pachacamac, a local pre-Inca deity who was later appropriated by them. Valera equates Pachacamac, "he who gives being to the earth," with the Creator God of the Bible. Viracocha, described variously in conflicting myths as a culture hero, a creator, or a rag-wearing wanderer, was identified by some writers as the apostle Bartholomew—again, an effort on the part of the Spanish to fit the Americas into salvation history and, in this case, to account for the positive fulfillment of Christ's command to his apostles to "make disciples of all nations." For Valera, however, Viracocha was Pachacamac in human flesh—in other words, Christ. He went so far as to translate the word *Viracocha* with the Latin *numen*, the "will and power of God." Valera continues to explain Inca polytheism as an error, nonetheless, in which the Peruvians began to worship the attributes of the true God under the forms of the stars, moon, and planets.

The points of commonality between Catholic traditions and Inca religion are in themselves unremarkable. It was somewhat common practice for missionaries to take note of such parallels in order to develop points of contact between the two for the purposes of evangelism or even to raise the dignity of indigenous spirituality to the level of pre-Christian anticipation. This did not prevent them from seeking to destroy the physical elements of native religion as corrupted by demonic influence. Valera, however, went further by ascribing Peruvian religion not simply to the natural religious instincts possessed by all human beings or even to some primordial preaching of the gospel by a wave-tossed apostle. Rather, in identifying Pachacamac with the Hebrew God and Viracocha with Christ, he raises the Inca tradition to the status of divine revelation.

This threatened to skirt too closely to heresy as it denied the unique revelation of God in the historic Jesus of Nazareth. Additionally, it approximated treason. The special revelation of the God-made-flesh to the Inca would completely subvert one of the primary justifications for the Spanish conquest, that of bringing Light to the spiritually blind, and consequently undermine the entire colonial enterprise. After 1583 Valera would suffer exile and numerous imprisonments for reasons that remain unclear, culminating in his banishment from Peru in 1596 and death a year later.

Over a half century later, the Mexican poet and polymath Sor Juana Inés de la Cruz (1648–1695) revisited the question of Indian religion in the introductory poem (*loa*) to her play *The Divine Narcissus*, intended for the Spanish court.[4] Though a cloistered nun for most of her adult life, she was greatly aware of the mixed populace of Mexico City and was able to reproduce the languages, accents, and dialects she had encountered as a lady-in-waiting. By giving voice to the indigenous and African peoples outside her walls, through her poetry Sor Juana was able to critique the conquest and exploitation of others in a way that she never could through a straightforward denunciation.

In the prologue, Juana crafts a conversation between Occident and America (both Indians) and Religion and Zeal (representing Roman Catholicism and the Spanish military, respectively). America and Occident celebrate the feast of the god of the harvest, using language analogous to Christianity.

> Moreover, his protection
> is not restricted to nurture
> of material food,
> but later by eating

---

4. Material in this section was originally published in Joel Morales Cruz, *The Mexican Reformation* (Eugene, OR: Wipf and Stock, 2010), 65–67.

his very own flesh
(purified in advance
of bodily dross),
we may be cleansed of the
stains on our souls.[5]

Upon entering, Religion attempts to convert them to Christianity, but when they refuse, Zeal threatens them. The conquest (Zeal) is presented as brash and irrational while Religion seeks to persuade America and Occident to convert through reason, convincing them that their religions were anticipations of Christianity, celebrated through the Eucharist. At the conclusion of the *loa* Juana pushes the envelope further, seemingly equating the Christian God with the Indian "God of the Seeds." America, Occident, and Zeal sing:

As we say, already
the Indies know
who is the true
God of the Seeds!
And with tender tears
that pleasure distills,
let us joyfully repeat
with festive voice;

ALL

Blessed be the day
I came to know the great God of the Seeds![6]

Without detracting from the necessity of completing native faith through Catholic evangelization, Sor Juana nonetheless gave voice to the indigenous people before the royal court and, in effect, sought to evangelize the Spanish on the dignity of native traditions, placing

---

5. Pamela Kirk Rappaport, *Sor Juana Inés de la Cruz: Selected Writings* (Mahwah, NJ: Paulist, 2005), 71.
6. Ibid., 88.

it on par with Greco-Roman religion as prefiguring Christianity. She subversively, if not altogether unsubtly, criticizes the wars of conquest with their stated aim of saving the Indians from idolatry, arguing instead for a greater understanding of Indian religion, evangelization through persuasion and peace, and the very possibility that the Indians had been worshipping the true God all along.

2:2:3: "God Has Not Done Likewise to Any Other Nation"

One result of the Catholic Enlightenment in Latin America was the growth of an incipient nationalism due in part to new historiographical approaches, the growth of new sciences such as archaeology, and, perhaps most importantly, the appropriation of religious symbols to foster a distinct Creole patriotism.[7] Colonial society was highly structured according the concept of *limpieza de sangre*. Spain's preoccupation with maintaining racial and religious purity without the taint of Jewish or Arab blood had been imported and adapted for the New World. Whites stood at the apex, after which followed the various castes or racial combinations descending according to perceived whiteness or lack thereof. Indians and blacks formed the bottom of this social pyramid. Whites were divided into two categories, those born in Europe and the Creoles born in the Americas. European-born Spaniards held most of the highest positions within the government and the church. One reason was practical. Those coming from Spain identified with their homeland and were thought to better maintain their allegiance to the Crown. Another reason lay with stereotypical perceptions based on birthplace. The American heat and humidity was thought to determine Creole character, born to be idle, shiftless, physically weak,

---

7. Adapted from Cruz, *Mexican Reformation*, 109–18.

and less intelligent. These attitudes, and the exclusion of Creoles from society's highest offices, created an animosity and resentment between the two groups. This accusation was echoed by Antonio Joaquín de Rivadeneira, a Creole lawyer and member of the *audiencia* in Mexico, who wrote in 1771:

> It is not the first time that the reputation of the Americans has been maliciously attacked and that they have been regarded as unsuitable for honors of any kind. This is a war we have suffered since the discovery of America. The Indians, the natives born and originating in America, have even had their rationality questioned, against all the evidence. With equal injustice it is also claimed that those of us born here of European ancestry lack enough reason to be really men. We have been depicted as suspicious creatures, full of our own opinions, resentful of reproof, and—the ultimate insult—it has been alleged that Mexico is apparently moribund.[8]

By 1700 the children of the conquistadors were facing disappointment. They were simply not the lords of the land as their ancestors had hoped. The high mortality rate of the Indian population along with the animosity of the Crown had reduced the value of *encomiendas*. Further, newly arrived immigrants had become successful in silver mining and overseas commerce. In reaction, Creoles looked to the conquest and, more specifically, to its critics such as Bartolomé de Las Casas, and they concluded that "the crimes of the conquerors were punished in the poverty and misery of their descendants." In addition to lamenting the sins of the fathers, this new generation of Creoles lifted up the Indian past, comparing Aztec society, for example, to classical antiquity, noting that despite their bloody religion, the Aztecs had, as visible in their laws and ruins, attained true civilization. Creole apologists would return to the

---

8. Antonio Joaquin de Rivadeneira, "America for the Americans," quoted in Cruz, *Mexican Reformation*, 109–10.

indigenous past again and again, forming a mythical bridge, as it were, between themselves and the Aztecs and Maya.

A decidedly Catholic interpretation of the history of New Spain contributed to the rise of Creole pride and nationalism. We have noted above how early explorers and missionaries sought to reconcile the Bible with the peoples and civilizations they encountered. The similarities between Christianity and indigenous religion demanded a genetic relationship. Cruciform shapes, confession, fasting, and circumcision as well as the belief in one Creator God, in a virgin miraculously made mother, and in the universal deluge all pointed in that direction. Blas Valera had identified Viracocha with Christ, and others focused on the person of Quetzalcóatl, the plumed-serpent god and the mythic king of the Toltecs who had taught the people agriculture and culture. Missionaries took hold of these legends to propose an apostolic evangelization of the Americas. After all, did not some images of Quetzalcóatl show the god wearing a cross on his mantle? And did not his name figuratively mean "precious twin?" Taking these clues, Carlos Sigüenza y Góngora (1645–1700), a contemporary and friend of Sor Juana Inés de la Cruz, linked Quetzalcóatl to Saint Thomas, whose Greek name, Didymus, means "twin."

According to what became popular legend, Thomas, after evangelizing India, made his way to the Americas where he preached the gospel. For Creoles this link was extremely important. Spain and other European nations claimed for themselves some form of apostolic pedigree from the apostles Peter and Paul in Rome to Joseph of Arimethea in England to Saint James in Spain. Between the religious categories of Christians and unbelievers was the inferior and spiritually dependent category of newly converted barbarian. Was not Spanish society in the Renaissance divided between "old Christians" and *conversos*, persons who had converted, or whose recent ancestors had converted, from Islam or Judaism? And spiritual subjection led to political subjection. The New World's apostolic credentials in the biblical saint could bypass the violence of the conquest and allow the American people to change their spiritual status and stand as equals by their European brethren.

A more potent figure stands in the center of the religious roots of Mexican nationalism, however. In 1648, Miguel Sánchez (d. 1674), a popular preacher and chaplain, wrote a tract known as the *Imagen de la Virgen María* (Image of the Virgin Mary). Written in Spanish, this account of the 1531 apparition subverts the prerogatives assumed by the Europeans by recreating the Spanish apparition stories on American soil. Designed to appeal to Creole feelings toward the Mexican homeland, it raises the question of how the New World and the Creole people could be inferior to the European when the Virgin Mary herself has appeared in Mexico as a native of the land. A year later, the *Nican Mopohua*, the Nahua account of the apparition of the Virgin of Guadalupe to the Indian Juan Diego Cuauhtlatoatzin (1474–1548) written by Luis Laso de la Vega, would further subvert the myth by returning it to its indigenous roots. A popular object of devotion since the sixteenth century among Creoles and Indians, this American Madonna was extolled in poems, panegyrics, and sermons. The laud given to the Virgin of Tepeyac Hill would come to fruition in her assignation as patron saint of New Spain by Pope Benedict XIV in 1756.

The Virgin of Guadalupe represented a founding myth, the spiritual establishment of the Mexican church and nation. She chose to appear to an Indian and in the brown skin of an Indian, magnifying the American quality of the story. Implicitly, Mary's apparition undermined the peninsular roots of the church, connecting the people of Mexico—the Indians and the Creoles—with a spiritual lineage that went far beyond apostolic credentials. Indeed, the Latin inscription attributed to her from Psalm 147:20—"non fecit taliter omni nationi" (she has not done this for any other nation)—dates from this era and attests to Mexico's favored place in the spiritual economy.[9] Here one poet compares her apparition with that given to John, the author of the book of Revelation.

> The world wonders,
> Heaven, the birds, angels and men
> Suspend their echoes,
> Hold still their voices
> That in New Spain
> From another John is heard
> A new Apocalypse,
> Although the revelations differ.
> From America in the desert,
> And in the crags of a hill,
> Patmos of New Spain
> Hides another John. . . .
> A great Sign in the heavens
> Of Guadalupe, there unfolds
> A Conception in roses,
> Which has idols at her feet. . . .[10]

Further research, carried on by Carlos de Sigüenza y Góngira (1645–1700) and others into the Guadalupe story and into Mexico's pre-Columbian past not only resulted in the birth of Mesoamerican archaeology during the Enlightenment but also gave Creoles sufficient scholarly tools to assert their own distinct patriotism and to dismiss remaining assertions of American inferiority, weakness, or corruption.

---

9. Though the Latin of the inscription is neuter and could refer to God, writers of the era frequently translated it in reference to Mary.
10. By Felipe de Santoyo García quoted in D. A. Brading. *Mexican Phoenix: Our Lady of Guadalupe; Image and Tradition across Five Centuries* (Cambridge: Cambridge University Press, 2001), 99–101.

The reforms of Charles III in the latter half of the eighteenth century placed a spotlight on the administration of the Americas. The Bourbon monarch insisted on the Americas' submissive status as colonies to enrich the mother country. Emboldened by a new sense of patriotism, Creoles called for a change in the dominant system, asking that American Spaniards be appointed to the highest ranks and railing against *peninsulares* who came to America to govern with no previous knowledge of the lands, customs, laws, or peoples. Against crude stereotypes of the Americas, Creole elites both at home and abroad appealed to the natural wonders of the Americas and to the civilizations of the Aztec and Inca peoples as equal to Europe's. The resentment over absolutist claims favoring European Spaniards was exacerbated with the expulsion of the Jesuits in 1767. Some resisted the command and sought to defend the members of the order, suffering penalties, in some cases severe. The decree resulted in several riots in missions and wherever the Jesuits were popular, especially among the Creole elite, many of whom had been educated in Jesuit schools.

A figure that ties many of these threads together, the religious and the patriotic, was Fray Servando Teresa de Mier (1765–1827). This Dominican priest, controversial in his own time, straddles colonial New Spain and the early Mexican republic. He exemplifies the religious side of Creole Mexican nationalism, rooted in his particular interpretations of the Guadalupe story and its ramifications for public life. Additionally, his arguments as well as the reflections contained in his memoirs bring to light the mirror side of Spanish regalism: the desire for the colonies to gain independence and to develop a Mexican church.

As a young man, Teresa de Mier was called to preach before the viceroy, archbishop, and Mexican dignitaries on the feast day of Our Lady of Guadalupe in 1794 at her newly restored sanctuary. Here he delivered a monumental sermon, a turning point that would forever alter his path. Mounting the pulpit, Fray Servando put forth four propositions that stunned his audience:

- The image of Guadalupe had been imprinted on the mantle of Thomas and not on the *tilma* of Juan Diego.
- Saint Thomas had hidden the image after the Indians had fallen into apostasy.
- The Virgin Mary had indeed appeared to Juan Diego but to reveal to him the whereabouts of the image.
- The Guadalupe image was still miraculous in origin, as the Virgin, while still alive, had imprinted it on St. Thomas's mantle.

The ramifications were obvious to his listeners. By moving the apparition from the more recent colonial past to the first century, the friar had given New Spain an apostolic and supernatural credential that was the very equal of, if not superior to, any in Europe. Further, by asserting that the Mexican church had been established in the years immediately after Christ's death and resurrection, as was visible in the relics and antiquities of the Aztecs recently unearthed that demonstrated Thomas as Quetzalcóatl, Servando undermined the entire Spanish colonial enterprise. If the apostle had evangelized the Americas with the miraculous image of Mary herself, what need was there for the conquest and subsequent occupation and colonization of the Americas? Teresa de Mier ended his sermon invoking the Virgin with the titles of Aztec goddesses: "Teotenantzin entirely Virgin, trustworthy Tonacayona . . . Flowery Coyolxauhqui, true Coatlicue de Minjó."[11]

---

11. Brading, *Mexican Phoenix*, 204.

Jailed and exiled, Fray Servando spent several years in Europe where he came to support the French Revolution and, later, the Mexican insurgency of 1810. He publically called into question the donations of Pope Alexander of 1493 and argued that the papal monarchy was based on forged documents such as the Donation of Constantine. It had become obvious to him that the papacy had no right or authority to condone the conquest. In other words, the Mexicans were only taking back what was rightfully theirs.

2:3: The Early Republics: "Is It Right to Pay Taxes to Caesar?"

The dawn of the nineteenth century was marked by cries of independence throughout Spanish America beginning in 1810. The French invasion of Spain in 1808 and the deposition of Fernando VII caused a crisis of authority throughout the New World that led to multiple insurgencies against the colonial governments. Inspired by the revolutions in the United States and Haiti, individuals such as Simón Bolívar in Venezuela, José de San Martín of Argentina, and the Mexican priest Miguel Hidalgo led the struggle for self-government. Some of these movements, like the one led by Hidalgo, were temporarily successful in marshalling the poor, Indians, and free blacks in search of a more equitable society. Most represented the political and economic interests of the Creole elite. By 1825, all of Spanish America, with the exception of Cuba and Puerto Rico, were independent. Brazil had achieved a constitutional monarchy in 1822. As Roman Catholic nation-states, the new republics not only needed an ideological foundation on which to govern and international recognition but also a theological argument to justify rebellion against the Spanish Crown.

The crux of the matter lay with the New Testament text admonishing believers to submit to the governing authorities.[12] This passage was troublesome both to those who believed in the divine right of kings as well as to those who held that the sovereignty of the people had ceded some authority to the state. Rebellion against divinely constituted and lawful authority was rebellion against God. When Miguel Hidalgo led armies of peasants across central Mexico, holding the standard of the Virgin of Guadalupe, Archbishop Manuel Abad y Quiepo, who had long advocated on behalf of those exploited by the colonial structures, excommunicated the priest and charged him with heresy. Fray Servando, writing from London, cautioned against too literal an interpretation of the Romans text, arguing that divinely ordained authority was meant neither to turn monarchs into demigods nor to usurp the natural rights of the people or their social contracts. Similarly, the Chilean Franciscan José María Bazaguchiascua (d. 1840) turned the regalist argument from Romans on its head. Writing in 1828, he stated that governments receive their legitimacy from the collective will of the people. If the Chilean people had opted for a democratic state against an absolutist monarchy, then that selfsame government was legitimate before God and any resistance to the popular will was sinful. Gregorio de Funes, writing from Argentina in 1814, affirmed that all human beings, coming from a common origin, were granted by God the ability to create orderly societies for the common good. He believed in the providential nature of the Spanish discovery of America but lamented the exploitation of the colonies by ambitious kings who used religion to justify and enforce their power. For Funes, then, the independence movements came to represent not only a return to the Divine Will

12. "Let every person be subject to the governing authorities; for there is no authority except from God, and those authorities that exist have been instituted by God. Therefore whoever resists authority resists what God has appointed, and those who resist will incur judgment" (Rom. 13:1-2).

but also a new age that in accordance with Eternal Wisdom, replaced the despotism of kings with the will of the people.

Nonetheless, the nascent republics recognized early on the ecclesiastical crisis brought on by independence. Episcopal sees throughout Latin America were vacant, the bishops, many born in Spain, having abandoned their dioceses or been forced into exile as a result of their opposition to the insurgency. It was imperative that the Vatican recognize the new nations, both to resolve this crisis and to facilitate political and economic relationships with other countries. Some countries sent delegates to the Vatican, hoping to form concordats with the papacy. Others, including Peru and Colombia, sought to abrogate to themselves the royal patronage and use that power to pressure the pope into accepting their episcopal candidates.

2:3:1: The Question of Patronage

One of the most contentious issues of nineteenth-century Latin America was the fate of the *patronato real,* the traditional right of the Spanish monarch to name bishops to vacant episcopal sees. Since the Catholic Enlightenment, Gallican and Jansenist ideas had been circulating throughout Spain and Latin America, raising questions as to whether the church existed as a body transcending borders with the pope as its spiritual and temporal head, or whether the administration of the church lay within the power and responsibilities of the monarch with the pope as a purely spiritual leader.[13] At the conclusion of the wars of independence, the question of whether

---

13. Gallican and Jansenist movements, both from France, asserted the power of the state over the administrative affairs of the church within its borders. It is contrasted with ultramontanism ("across the mountains," that is, the Alps) that held to the power of the pope in all matters related to the Catholic Church.

patronage resided in the government of the new republics or reverted back to the papacy was critical to church-state relations and to the survival of the Catholic Church. In this pre–Vatican I era before the centralization of the Catholic Church around the figure of the pope, clergy were divided in their perspectives on the relationship between the national churches, the state, and the Vatican.

In Mexico, for example, one priest, Rafael Abogado (d.1828), repeated the Thomistic affirmation that the head of the church is Christ, whose vicar on earth is the pope. In an 1826 pamphlet he defends the superiority of the pope above all other bishops, and, though he is a convinced monarchist as regards secular governance, his emphasis on papal authority over the church leads him to come down hard in support of the pope having the privilege of appointing bishops.

José Ignacio Moreno (1767–1841) of Ecuador wrote in 1831 against Gallican impulses within society that would seek to limit the power of the pope over the church. He asked whether the office of the bishops was merely an administrative role delegated by the papacy. Broadly interpreting Luke 22:32, he concluded that the authority of the bishops found its source in Christ through the keys of Peter—that is, the pope.[14]

On the other side of the spectrum stood Fray Servando once again. After Mexico won its independence, Teresa de Mier was apprehensive about establishing relations with the papacy. While acknowledging the spiritual authority of the pope, he nonetheless presented the French Constitution of 1791 as appropriate for Mexico, arguing that the people should vote for their bishops and that each diocese had the power to consecrate them without referring to Rome. He advocated the establishment of a national Catholic Church in

---

14. "But I have prayed for you that your own faith may not fail; and you, when once you have turned back, strengthen your brothers" (Luke 22:32).

which Mexicans would elect their own episcopate. His fears appeared justified when in 1824 Pope Leo XII issued an encyclical exhorting Spanish Americans to renew their allegiance to the Spanish king. Fray Servando excoriated the papacy's meddling in political affairs, reminding his readers that the Vatican had unleashed violence and murder in the Americas through the Alexandrine donations.

2:3:2: New Christendom

The latter part of the nineteenth century was generally characterized by political and ideological struggles between Conservatives and Liberals. Throughout much of the continent, Liberal administrations took the upper hand from the 1880s on. They implemented a program of modernization: enacting religious liberty; secularizing birth, marriage, and death records; and instituting public education. The South American republics in particular revoked many of the church's traditional privileges (such as ecclesiastical courts) and abolished the tithe, collected from the public in order to sustain the church financially. Instead, Liberal governments put the clergy on the national payroll, effectively making the church a department of the state. In the extreme instance of Paraguay, this became a de facto presidential theology. During the successive presidencies of José Gaspar Rodríguez de Francia, Carlos Antonio López, and their relative, Francisco Solanos López, the Catholic Church was reduced to a state of servitude. Tolerating no competition to their authority, they sought to combat the church's hold over the people on a symbolic, yet very real level. An 1845 decree outlawed traditional acts of reverence toward the bishops, such as kneeling or ringing church bells. It also forbade the bishops from using the episcopal throne or official vestments. Under Solanos López, the divine right of the president became a tenet of the faith to be preached in the churches and taught in catechisms. As a result, the church became an ideological tool of the government that would promise heavenly rewards for those who fought during Paraguay's utterly disastrous war against Argentina, Brazil, and Uruguay.

Yet change was in the wind. Freedom of religion came first as the rights of conscience gradually or abruptly was extended from foreigners to the citizenry. By the third decade of the twentieth century, most Latin American republics had disestablished the church, removing it from its traditional role as state religion. Whether this separation reverberated in violence as in Mexico or occurred peacefully and matter-of-factly as in Uruguay and Chile, the church was forced to come to terms with a new social, political, and ecclesiastical reality.

New Christendom, dating to the beginnings of the 1930s, was the Catholic Church's attempt to redefine its ministry in the modern era. It began by recognizing the separation of the spiritual and temporal realms and then sought to bring them closer by interacting only indirectly with the state through lay organizations and individuals and by strengthening private and familial piety.

This new way of interacting with the world has its foundations in the social encyclicals of the Catholic Church and in the thought of the French philosopher Jacques Maritain (1882–1973). In 1891, Pope Leo XIII issued *Rerum Novarum*, a document that recognizes the needs and rights of labor in the face of expanding industrialization and rising socialism and approves of the formation of private unions in order to collectively bargain for better working conditions. The encyclical gave rise to the Christian Democracy movement throughout Europe and Latin America and the formation of Catholic Action in 1931, both programs urging laypeople to apply Catholic social principles to the workplace, the university, politics, and labor unions.

Maritain, in distinguishing between the spiritual and temporal, asserted that neither could be separated from the other. Nonetheless, each is autonomous within its own realm, the temporal within the order of nature (culture, law, justice) and the spiritual within that of grace, perfecting or fulfilling the natural order (as per Aquinas) so that the temporal can achieve the best common good. The relationship is symbiotic: the church works best within a well-ordered society to bring people to salvation, whereas the state, as product of fallen human nature, needs God's grace in order to operate at its best. This does not mean that the state can usher in the kingdom of God through the church's intervention. The establishment of justice, rule of law, human rights, and the like only produces the positive context for the church in which to operate and preach the gospel. The kingdom of God remains an eschatological vision.

Though the New Christendom model took particular root throughout South America, not everyone became enamored of it. Julio Meinvielle (1905–1973), an Argentinian priest and writer, began to attack Jacques Maritain's assumptions beginning in 1936 when the latter visited Argentina. A far-right conservative, Meinvielle believed that by distinguishing between the temporal and spiritual spheres Maritain had succumbed to the errors of modernism and had surrendered the church to the secular world. Meinvielle was among those theologians who, basing himself on the work of Thomas Aquinas, looked to a return of the medieval model of the church and state. He was an enemy of materialist capitalism, Marxism, and the Jews, on whom he faulted whatever ills the Christian world suffered. Meinvielle believed that in the struggle for Christian civilization, which he described in apocalyptic terms against the Jewish people, Christians must strive for unity and, if necessary, use violence for the sake of the truth. To that end, he was an advocate of nationalist fascism.

In Chile, Alberto Hurtado (1901–1952) became an outspoken critic of the failures of the New Christendom. Hurtado worked as professor of religion, analyzing the state of religion in Chile even while immersing himself in the cause of the poor. The fruits of his first endeavor are seen in his book *Is Chile a Catholic Country?* (1941), an analysis of the country's socioeconomic situation that pointed out the shortage of priests assigned to rural and working-class populations and took the church to task for its neglect of the poor and the substandard education of its priests. In return he was criticized by the conservative hierarchy and accused of being a communist. Throughout the 1940s, Hurtado wrote several books touching on social humanism and the Catholic response to concerns of labor.

Victor Belaúnde (1883–1966) was a conservative thinker who, along the lines of the Spanish thinker Americo Castro, looked to an arguably romanticized past to meet the challenges of Peru's present. He believed that, despite its shortcomings, Peru represented the perfect synthesis of Spanish and Indian cultures. Integral to that society was Catholicism. He saw in the social papal encyclicals a blueprint for the just society and spent his political and educational career seeking to make them a reality in Peru. However, he sidestepped one of the distinguishing features of the New Christendom. Believing that Catholicism transcends political causes, he rejected the idea of a "Catholic" political party.

The proposed model of the church being in the world was not followed uniformly throughout Latin America. As Catholic parties gained power and influence, the church itself began to form alliances with the state. In the end, the New Christendom began to strongly resemble the old one.

2:3:3: The Protestant Vision

Protestant missionaries began entering Latin America in the 1820s. At first, they came primarily from Great Britain—Anglicans, Methodists, Bible society colporteurs. However, they were soon overtaken by missionaries from the United States. Geographical proximity, coupled with the evangelistic zeal arising from the Second Great Awakening and the later Student Volunteer Movement for Foreign Missions, made Latin America a prime mission field. One must also not discount the military, economic, and ideological expansionist energies pulsating throughout the United States in the nineteenth century. Early Protestantism was conversionist in nature; that is, as heirs of the Reformation, they perceived Roman Catholicism as superstitious, backward, enslaving, and ultimately something from which Latin Americans needed to be rescued. The missionaries who brought with them an emphasis upon the biblical word, justification by faith, iconoclasm, and the individual's unmediated relationship with God were also agents of their culture, freely mixing their sociopolitical assumptions with their religious convictions as surely as the first Spanish missionaries had done centuries earlier. Freedom was often translated into the socioeconomic sphere as individualism, the "Protestant work ethic," and capitalism; in politics, as democracy and republicanism. Protestant churches and missionaries generally favored and benefited from Liberal administrations as they advocated for religious freedom, the disestablishment of the Catholic Church, public education, and increased economic relationships with the United States.

Beginning in the 1920s, the Protestant churches in Latin America began a process of transformation. A generation of native leaders buckled under the often-paternalistic attitudes of the missionaries and sought to gain some control over their own churches, efforts that sometimes resulted in bitter feuds, schisms, and the establishment of national Presbyterian, Methodist, Baptist, and Pentecostal denominations. In this groundswell, Latin American Protestants began to discover their voice and to interpret the tradition through their own experiences and national contexts.

One of the challenges that Protestants often faced was the accusation that their faith was a foreign import at odds with Latin American identity itself, so intertwined with Catholicism. Protestants were accused of being agents or dupes of US imperialism and traitors to their people. The Mexican American writer Alberto Rembao (1895–1962) answered some of these charges, rooting the Protestant Reformation itself in sixteenth-century Spanish figures such as Juan de Valdés and asserting that the Protestant spirit is that of liberty, a universal value. This liberty may have been nurtured by the Anglo-Saxon countries after being smothered in Spain by the Inquisition, but by the time Protestant missionaries arrived in Latin America, the region had already been filled with the spirit of liberty through the independence movements. The coming together of Latin American liberalism with the Protestant spirit was thus a match made in Heaven.

The relationship between liberal values and Protestantism can be seen in the participation of Protestants in the Mexican Revolution (1910–1920). Fearful that the reforms of the past half century would be eroded after the end of the Díaz regime, Protestants, particularly Methodists, began supporting the revolution. Eventually, many came to sympathize with the revolutionaries seeking land reforms and workers' rights. José Rumbia (1865–1913), an anti-Catholic Methodist pastor, preached to and helped organize textile workers. Writing in 1906, he excoriated the intellectual classes, the *científicos*, for the "lack of disposition among those men of culture and learning to teach and to propagate good ideas on behalf of those whom we call 'the common people'" and argued that "light and liberty seem to have been made solely for those of high birth and who have the privilege of monopolizing knowledge as if it were any other commodity." He further attacked those who exploited the economy, both foreign and domestic, as "more greedy than patriotic, who desire everything even if the entire world were lost."[15]

The yearning on the part of church leaders and some missionaries to overcome the fragmentation that is endemic to Protestantism and to set forth Latin Americanized churches and denominations resulted in a number of ecumenical meetings in the first half of the twentieth century. The 1916 Congress of Panama was dominated by North Americans, who determined the agenda and even the language of the proceedings, English. Despite this, they concentrated on the sociopolitical hindrances to the spread of the gospel and called for the development of socially conscious autonomous churches and an expansion of the role of women in society. A larger Latin American contingent participated in the Montevideo Conference of 1925, but it remained controlled by foreign missionaries. Here, a greater emphasis on the social gospel was spelled out, with the "Fatherhood of God, the centrality of Christ, and the necessity of repentance," a gospel that called individuals not only to salvation but also to social regeneration. Socioeconomic problems produced by industrialized capitalist sectors, temperance, women's rights, and workers' rights remained under discussion. By this time, tensions between liberals and fundamentalists had evolved into full-on opposition in the United States and were reflected in Montevideo among some of the delegates who questioned the conference's social emphasis.

---

15. José Rumbia, "Y dijo Dios, la Luz sea y la Luz fue," ACI, September 13, 1906, 302–3, as quoted in Jean-Pierre Bastian, *Los disidentes: Sociedades protestantes y revolución en México, 1872–1911* (Mexico City: Fondo de Cultura Económica, 1989), 240–41. Translation by the author.

It was not until Havana, in 1929, that Latin American nationals were able to control the proceedings of the conference, marking a turning point toward the transformation of Protestantism on the continent. A body of highly educated leaders as well as nationalist and populist impulses rippling from the Mexican Revolution fostered a central desire to contextualize Protestantism, often resulting in anti-American and anti-imperialist sentiments. Addressing the concern that Protestants represented a sort of fifth column for US economic and political interests (particularly in light of the Spanish-American War and recent military interventions in Cuba, the Dominican Republic, Nicaragua, and Panama), the delegates voiced their desire to distance themselves from the US missionary effort in favor of truly national, autonomous churches. These were to be thoroughly Latinized, not just in name but in ideology and practice, rooted within the needs, challenges, and cultures of the region. However, some delegates closer to the United States, such as Alberto Rembao, lamented the general anti-American sentiment, and others saw this swing toward nationalism and social concerns as symptoms of bolshevism, presaging some of the divisions within the Latin American churches decades later.

2:4: Modern Period:
"What Shall We Do to Be Saved?"

Beginning in the late 1950s, military dictatorships began taking control of many countries from Argentina to Guatemala. Conservative and anticommunist, they were supported by the United States, especially after the Cuban Revolution placed a Soviet satellite at its doorstep. These military regimes quickly turned repressive and violent, resulting in the disappearances and deaths of thousands through the 1980s. The power of these undemocratic states essentially spelled defeat to the New Christendom model. In many regions, church hierarchies rushed toward new deals with the states in order to protect their interests and guarantee a modicum of liberty to minister to the people. Some members of Catholic Action became conservative defenders of the status quo; others—laypeople, clergy, and members of the religious orders—became more radicalized. Meanwhile, the Second Vatican Council (1962–1965) was trying to bring the church into the modern age, emphasizing the essentiality of the laity, proposing new models for the church, and encouraging bishops and theologians to contextualize the gospel within their local needs and challenges. The historic Protestant churches, meanwhile, continued the efforts to define themselves apart from their missionary roots. The Pentecostals, having begun as a trickle at the start of the century, now stood poised to become one of the most important religious movements of the era.

2:4:1: Liberation Theology

Liberation theology began as a response to the gripping socioeconomic and political problems facing Latin America that left millions entrenched in poverty and need while benefiting the very few. Several streams converged in the formation of this new expression of defining the gospel and its mission. Radicalized members of Catholic Action, priests, and members of religious orders had already been working among the urban and rural poor and were intimate with their needs. University students and educators, attached to the pedagogical theories of Paulo Freire (1921–1997), sought to raise the consciousness of the masses, and a new generation of theologians, educated in Europe, returned with the sociological tools to critically reflect on political, economic, and social problems of the region. From the 1960s, Christian base communities (CEB) began to organize among the ordinary people. Starting out as an effort to bring people together to reflect on the Scriptures within their everyday lives, CEBs became sources of political and social solidarity seeking to improve communities in the face of larger obstacles. At the 1968 meeting of CELAM in Medellín, the gathered bishops in essence rejected New Christendom in favor of a prophetic model for the church. Reflecting on the church's response to military repression and poverty and asking where God was in the suffering of the poor, they broke with four centuries of tradition, refusing to identify with those in power and instead proclaiming "God's preferential option for the poor." Rather than stressing the "opiate" of a post-death heavenly existence, the church began to emphasize God's saving work in the here and now, the breaking in of the eschatological kingdom through the reforming of societal structures and attitudes of oppression and discrimination to proclaim a holistic salvation that addresses the needs of the naked body and empty stomach as well as the spirit. The Exodus story became a key text, as did Jesus' words in Luke 4:

> The Spirit of the Lord is upon me,
> because he has anointed me
> to bring good news to the poor.
> He has sent me to proclaim release to the captives
> and recovery of sight to the blind,
> to let the oppressed go free,
> to proclaim the year of the Lord's favor.

Taking a page from Catholic Action, they flipped the traditional European emphasis on doctrine preceding action and stated that theological reflection begins with a process of seeing, judging, and acting. In seeing, one tries to understand and describe the context of liberation—the struggles of the poor, societal structures of oppression, and so forth. One judges the situation in light of Christian principles, the revelation of God in Jesus Christ, and the priorities of love and justice. Finally, one must act to change the lives of the oppressed for the better. This praxis is informed by the tools at hand: sociological analysis, biblical hermeneutics, philosophy, the reflections of the poor, and the like.

Gustavo Gutiérrez (1928–) became one of the movement's earliest architects in *A Theology of Liberation*. Medellín stated that praxis—that is, a commitment to the poor with whom God has already sided in historical action and the life of Jesus—comes before doctrine. Beginning with this, the Peruvian priest defines theology as reflection based on actions taken to end human misery. It is a reflection of the grassroots, coming from the experiences of the oppressed, and they become agents in their own liberation. Faith is encounter with God that moves one to accompany and identify with the poor in their struggles and to commit oneself to the reformation of sinful dispositions and institutions that keep people impoverished and subject to violence. Whereas in the New Christendom model social change set the stage for the message of salvation, for Gutiérrez liberation and salvation are synonymous, involving the structural, transforming societal institutions; the human, allowing people and communities to become agents in their own liberation; and the individual, the personal freedom one finds in Christ. He is nonetheless careful not to equate any political or societal changes with the incoming kingdom of God. Changes in government, institutions, and communities toward justice may be signs of the in-breaking reign of God, but they do not constitute it.

In their respective works, the Brazilian Leonardo Boff (1938–) and Jon Sobrino (1938–), writing from El Salvador, focus on the person of Christ. Both of them begin with the Jesus of history, the mission of the Nazarene within his historical context as a prophet addressing the everyday lives of the people under Roman oppression.

Boff thus places Jesus' preaching of the kingdom as it arrives in the here and now and asks what the kingdom of God looks like within the Latin American context. In his life, death, and vindication, Jesus inaugurates the kingdom of God. For Sobrino, the poor of the world are the crucified Jesus today. God's choosing of the outcast and marginalized demonstrates their role as the soteriological nexus for God's action in the world. In other words, there is no salvation outside of the poor, and the church must find its identity and purpose in serving them. Since God identifies with and chooses the rejected of the world as divine instruments, it follows for Sobrino that God does not reveal Godself to the powerful, the leaders of empire, or the holders of wealth. As a result, the Vatican admonished Sobrino in 2007, declaring his writings to be in error. A worse fate befell Boff after he wrote that the church betrayed the gospel in order to ally itself with the powerful. Silenced for a year in 1985, he came into conflict again in 1992 with John Cardinal Ratzinger, the future Benedict XVI, leading Boff to leave the Franciscan order.

José Miguez Bonino (1924–2012) represents the Protestant expression of liberation theology. Like Gutiérrez and others, he begins with an analysis of the Latin American context—namely, its violent history from the conquest to the present. He uses the same metaphors of God's reign as revealed within the prophets and the ministry of Jesus as one of justice toward the poor, and he challenges the church to determine its priorities, whether its power will be used on their behalf or against them. Thus, Christians are charged with the responsibility to discern and work toward a societal order that best reflects the justice of God's reign. Unlike Gutiérrez and other Catholic theologians, Bonino, as a Methodist, seeks to preserve the Protestant emphasis on God's priority in salvation and grace. He does not see the church's actions in working toward liberation as the eruption of the kingdom but as an ethical response to God's actions in Christ that anticipates the eschatological reign.

Liberation theology came under attack in the 1970s and 1980s from both inside and outside the churches. One of the central points on which it was critiqued was its use of Marxist tools to analyze society. Though some liberationists definitely threw their hat into that particular ring, theologians and pastors have asserted that their commitment is not to a revolutionary political ideology but to the radical actions of God in history, rooted in prayer and service to others. Liberation theology, unlike many North American and European spiritualities, does not dichotomize the spiritual and the secular but insists that God's salvation must incorporate all facets of human life. Marxist analysis could be used without its materialistic presuppositions or demand for violent uprising. Nonetheless, liberation theology unnerved Pope John Paul II and John Cardinal Ratzinger, who in various ways sought to undermine and suppress its influence in Latin America, whether through maintaining alliances with corrupt governments, denying the persecution of Christians in the region, silencing theologians, or replacing radical bishops with traditionalists. In the midst of the Cold War, liberation theology, with its critique of capitalism and US military interventions on behalf of right-wing governments, was considered dangerous enough to draw the attention of US intelligence. With its affinities to conservative politics and a belief in US exceptionalism, evangelical Protestants in the United States were also critical of liberationist thought, in some cases supporting dictators such as Efraín Ríos Montt in Guatemala, both overtly and through close relationships with fellow evangelicals in Central and South America.

Liberation theology since its inception was concerned with the political and economic structures that kept the masses in poverty through violence. However, as its thought developed in the ensuing decades, reflection on the structures of oppression brought other forms of systematic violence and discrimination to light. Catholic and Protestant women began to point out the second-class status of women in Latin American society and the suffering that wives, mothers, and daughters in particular are subjected to in the midst of war and poverty. Elsa Tamez (1950–), a Methodist theologian from Mexico, has made an extensive study of how negative stereotypes about women are reinforced through Latin American music, dance, and stories. She uses the story of Hagar from the book of Genesis to illustrate how women suffer from discrimination based on class, gender, and race and are nonetheless especially chosen of God. María Pilar Aquino (1956–) focuses on the violence women suffer during times of war. She perceives of theology as a socioecclesial transformative force that confronts the realities of oppression and injustice in order to create relationships free of exploitation and violence.

Other forms of liberation theology have sprouted throughout the world, each forming within the context of its own national and local social and economic structures and cultures. Indigenous people, Afro-Latins, and other marginalized groups have lent their particular voices seeking liberation in the midst of their own struggles. In the United States, feminist, black, Asian American, womanist, and GLBT expressions exploring the roots of gender, sexual, racial, and class discriminations have broken forth in the last several decades. Among the Hispanic communities of the United States, Latino/a theology has emerged as a force within academia and the churches. Virgilio Elizondo (1935–), a Mexican American priest and scholar, was one of its pioneers in his book *Galilean Jesus*, where he sees Jesus as the prophet of the marginalized. Approaching the life of Christ from the Mexican American experience, he stresses the principle that what is rejected by those in power is chosen by God. In *Guadalupe: Mother of the New Creation*, Elizondo draws out the Guadalupe stories, pointing to cultural mingling or *mestizaje* in the apparition as a signpost and evidence of God's continual unfolding of the divine presence among God's people. A Cuban Methodist, Justo González (1937–) was also one of the early exponents of Latino/a theology. In *Mañana: Christian Theology from a Hispanic Perspective*, he also expounds the concept of *mestizaje* and approaches the major Christian beliefs of the Trinity, the Incarnation, and salvation from a Hispanic point of view.

Though its methodologies and conclusions have often been challenged, liberation theology has transformed Christian thought, favoring larger community identity and needs over traditionally Eurocentric views of the autonomous self. It has given marginalized people throughout the world a voice within the context of neoliberal economic and political dominance. Its ethical call challenges theologians and others to reexamine principles of paternalism and individualism in light of what those on the periphery want, working toward the formation of a society of equals. Extending those social concerns to the whole of creation at the dawn of the twenty-first century, liberation theology contests the claims of a materialistic capitalism that attributes monetary value to persons and things in the interest of a liberated environment able to sustain all living beings.

2:4:2: Pentecostalism

Pentecostalism entered Latin America in the early twentieth century and has since exploded to become the largest and most rapidly growing Protestant tradition in the region. Because the tradition is decentralized, it is difficult to apply the distinctive beliefs of a particular group to the churches as a whole. Coming from the Holiness tradition, Pentecostalism shares beliefs common to most evangelical Christians: the Trinity, the humanity and deity of Christ, salvation by faith, and the necessity of a conversion experience.[16] Pentecostalism's distinctive beliefs are that individuals experience a work of grace subsequent to conversion in which they are "baptized in the spirit" and that the miraculous biblical gifts (healing, exorcism, prophecy, and so on) are present in the church today. Some groups believe that the baptism of the Spirit is evidenced by glossolalia. In general, Pentecostalism is conservative in its theology, holding to a premillennial dispensationalism as the result of early missionary efforts and continuing contact from the United States. The Scriptures are seen as inspired and inerrant.

Two families of Pentecostalism are dominant in Latin America: historic Pentecostalism and neo-Pentecostalism, or charismatic churches. The first emerged from the early missionary efforts of Pentecostal denominations such as the Assemblies of God, the United Pentecostal Church, and others. Neo-Pentecostal churches began to arise in the 1960s within their local contexts and do not have those ties to the historic traditions.[17]

Pentecostal churches can be described as grassroots congregations. Leadership does not flow from the top down but from the bottom up as leaders are either recognized by the church community or individuals, feeling a vocational call, establish their own congregations. Since leadership is determined by the presence of the Spirit, Pentecostal congregations tend to be far more egalitarian than those in established denominations, and in many churches there is no

16. Oneness Pentecostals reject the Trinity, believing that the persons of the Godhead are titles or phases of God.

17. In addition, of course, is the charismatic movement wherein the spiritual experiences associated with Pentecostalism (Spirit baptism, tongues, healing) began to manifest themselves within other Christian traditions—Roman Catholic, Baptist, Presbyterian, and so on. Some of these continue to exist within their own denominations, holding to their tradition's theological and liturgical distinctives, whereas other groups were expelled from their churches or left to form their own independent congregations.

barrier to women serving as ordained ministers. Because the center of the tradition is the spiritual experience, however, the personal revelation given to the charismatic minister may determine polity, inspire distinctive traditions (such as head coverings for women or vegetarianism), or influence biblical interpretation. The growth of megachurches in Guatemala, Brazil, El Salvador, Mexico, and elsewhere has often been the result of an individual responding to a vision or interior call to establish a new congregation. Because of these individuals' unique spiritual authority, there are often few systems of checks and balances surrounding them, sometimes leading to allegations of spiritual or sexual abuse, financial exploitation, and fraud.

Interpreters are divided as to Pentecostalism's role vis-à-vis society. On the one hand, the individualism encouraged by the focus on the spiritual experience and the eschatological worldview involving a premillennial return of Christ to save believers and judge the world may discourage any sort of sociopolitical transformation of society. After conversion, believers are expected to live as part of a community distinguishable by its moral standards and evangelistic focus. Outreach to those in need is expected but tends to be secondary to holy living and does not generally entail a systemic structural approach.

Conversely, others see the Pentecostal experience as empowering individuals to take strong stances affecting social issues. As the churches multiply, they foster communities of mutual support that often replace disintegrating social structures, especially in the anonymity of large cities. One result is personal transformation. Coming together around the tangible presence of God and reinforcing a strong moral code, Pentecostal churches often become an aid to repairing broken lives. A stronger work ethic may represent the path to advancement. Men who convert will stop smoking and drinking, reinvesting their time and wages into their families. Additionally, the faith subverts traditional Latin American machismo; spousal abuse may end, wives and girlfriends may be treated with greater respect, and children may be encouraged to continue their studies. In El Salvador, where gang violence is endemic, conversion is seen as the only way out and, with that, as a new beginning of life.

In Brazil, scholars have noted that Pentecostals act on the tradition's moral vision to become agents for social change—criticizing policies, running for office, and becoming part of leftist groups like the Workers' Party. Pentecostal politicians are supported by Pentecostal pastors. As this demographic grows, elected officials must now take into account their interests, from abortion to electric service in the favelas. In becoming part of a select, Spirit-filled community, members begin to see themselves as the inverse of how they are perceived in society. The grassroots nature of their congregations helps them acquire organizational skills while their self-consciousness as children of God and evangelistic witness give them confidence to assert themselves outside the church on behalf of moral, religious, and political values. In some areas, this has led to coalitions with not only other evangelical churches but also Roman Catholics, as they come together to present a united face on matters of moral and national debate such as same-sex marriage.

A different approach to social salvation has been observed in Guatemala, a country that is still recovering from a decades-long civil war and continues to be racked by violence. There, Pentecostalism has been deeply linked to citizenship in ways that are reminiscent of the Religious Right in the United States. However, unlike liberationists, who question and often call for the subversion of institutional structures in the quest for justice, or the US Religious Right, which sees political power as the key for moral transformation, Guatemalan Pentecostals rely on spiritual practices—prayer vigils, fasts, exorcism—to change society. Churches like El Shaddai, led by Harold Caballeros, appeal to a middle-class demographic that seeks social change in Guatemala. Christian morality and family values are viewed as the path to heal the nation and avert another bellicose catastrophe. Their cosmology, as is generally the case within Pentecostalism, is divided into God and the devil, the church and the world, the godly and the ungodly. Even though God's victory is assured at the end of days, while we live our days on Earth the supernatural forces of good and evil stand behind the structures, institutions, and even individuals of everyday life. Believers are participants in similar struggles within their own souls, often perceived as a pitched battle between God and the devil. Society, then, is a macrocosm of one's own spiritual conflict. The private struggle and the public one are intertwined in the sense that each affects the other. Thus, in order to bring salvation to the country, believers are enjoined to participate in this spiritual behind-the-scenes war through prayer, worship, and the like. Spiritual gifts such as healing and exorcism are additional tools to subvert the satanic order seeking to take control of self, community, and society.

The truth behind Pentecostal social engagement is both/and. Recalling that the tradition is hardly monolithic and represents a grassroots piety and organization, it is not surprising that beliefs and actions regarding the proper response to the world will vary from region to region and congregation to congregation. Pentecostals are socially engaged and distant, sectarian and uniting, otherworldly and rooted in the here and now. As they themselves would remind us from John 3, "The wind blows where it chooses. . . . So it is with everyone who is born of the Spirit."

2:5: Theology in Art

Historically, scholars have privileged theological documents in order to describe the nature of Christian thought. This, of course, leaves but a partial portrait: theology done by the elite, the literate, the educated. Increasingly, other sources (poetry, biographies, sermons, music, art) are being sought out to recover the voices of others, including women, slaves, and the illiterate, and to enlarge that picture. Below is a small sampling of how various forms of art also reveal theology.

Not only did ornate baroque churches seek to offer God the best in beauty, but they also sent a clear message of Catholic triumphalism. Few said it so grandiosely as the Church of São Francisco in Salvador, Brazil.

In the process of contextualizing the Christian message into native culture, artists mixed European and American motifs, subtly placing indigenous culture on par with the Spanish. In *The Last Supper* by the Quechua artist Marcos Zapata (c.1710–1773) in Cuzco Cathedral, Jesus and the disciples dine on guinea pig and drink *chicha*, a fermented drink made of maize or fruit and once used in Inca religious rituals.

Is the Virgin the mountain or is the mountain the Virgin? This representation of the silver-rich mountain of Potosí includes the painting's patrons in grateful prayer for their wealth. However, to the native Aymara and Quechua, the interposition of Mary with the mountain itself would identify the Mother of Christ with the Pachamama, the revered Earth Mother.

There are many black Christs venerated throughout Latin America. Some, like the black Christ of Esquipulas of Guatemala may be associated with Mesoamerican symbolism touching death, darkness, and the underworld. Elsewhere, these figures attracted African slaves who sought out a God who identified with their own color and suffering.

From the sixteenth century, priests would use simple carved figures of Christ and the saints as tools for evangelism. These *santos* became central in the spirituality of the Puerto Rican people, particularly as a clergy shortage resulted in less contact with the institutional church in rural areas. Today they are hallmarks of Puerto Rican folk culture.

Since 1531, the Virgin of Guadalupe has been a symbol of Mexican identity and the mixture of European and native cultures in the New World. Today she assures the presence of God in the challenges facing immigrants as they seek new lives in the United States as this mural in Chicago's Pilsen neighborhood attests.

3

Latin American Christianity

An Overview

3:1: Demographics

Population	611,390,868[1]
Ethnic makeup	White—73 percent
	Black—12 percent
	Amerindian—11 percent
	Other—4 percent
Religion	Roman Catholic—68 percent
	Protestant—18.1 percent
	Other—3.59 percent
	None / Not reported—9.38 percent

1. Numbers are based on population figures of Ibero-American countries and are thus restricted to the countries within our scope of interest. Published figures elsewhere often include the non-Iberian countries of the Americas and the Caribbean, thus accounting for a discrepancy in final tallies.

3:2: Timeline

Date	Latin American Christianity	World Events and Culture
12000–30000 B.C.E.		First humans arrive in the Americas.
6000–3000 B.C.E.		Agriculture in the Americas.
1300–1500 C.E.		Aztec and Inca empires emerge.
1492		Fernando and Isabel of Spain capture Granada. Columbus lands in the Caribbean.
1494		Treaty of Tordesillas divides the New World between Spain and Portugal. Da Vinci, *Madonna of the Rocks*
1502		First African slaves arrive in the New World. University of Wittenberg founded.
1508	Papal bull gives control of the church in the Spanish colonies to the Crown.	Michelangelo begins Sistine Chapel.
1511	Antonio de Montesinos protests the abuse of the Indians.	Michael Servetus executed in Calvin's Geneva. Grünewald, *Isenheim Altarpiece*
1513	First diocese in the New World established in Santo Domingo,	Juan Ponce de León lands in Florida. Vasco Nunez de Balboa becomes the first European to see the Pacific Ocean.
1514	Bartolomé de Las Casas begins his lifelong defense of the Indians.	Pineapples arrive in Europe.
1517		Luther ignites the Protestant Reformation. Coffee brought to Europe.
1519		Charles I of Spain elected Holy Roman emperor. Leonardo da Vinci dies.
1521		Aztecs fall to Hernán Cortéz.

1524	First Franciscan missionaries arrive in Mexico.	Peasants' Revolt takes place in southern Germany. Turkeys introduced in Europe.
1531	The Virgin of Guadalupe appears to Juan Diego Cuauhtlatoatzin.	Henry VIII becomes head of the Church of England. University of Granada founded.
1532		Conquest of Peru begins. Sugar cane cultivated in Brazil.
1537	Pope Paul III declares the Indians to be fully human in *Sublimus Dei*.	
1541		Santiago de Chile founded. El Greco born. Viceroyalty of Peru established.
1542		New laws promulgated to protect Indians.
1545–1563		Council of Trent held.
1551	First Council of Lima, Peru, begins organizing Latin American church.	University of Mexico opens.
1570	Inquisition established in Peru.	The pope excommunicates Elizabeth I of England.
1571	Inquisition established in Mexico.	Johann Kepler born.
1580–1640		Spain and Portugal united.
1588		Spanish Armada falls. Vatican library founded.
1607		Jamestown founded.
1609	First Jesuit mission established in Paraguay.	Henry Hudson explores Delaware Bay.
1617	Rosa de Lima dies.	Pocahontas dies.
1620	Diocese of Buenos Aires founded.	Pilgrims land in Massachusetts.
1655		English seize Jamaica.
1700		Charles II, last of the Spanish Hapsburgs, dies; Bourbons take the Spanish throne.

1701-1714		War of Spanish Succession.
1754–1763		Seven Years' War fought.
1759–1788	Catholic Enlightenment in the Americas occurs.	Charles III rules Spain.
1767	Jesuits expelled from the Spanish colonies.	
1776	Junipero Serra founds San Francisco.	United States declares independence. Adam Smith, *Wealth of Nations*
1780–1781		Tupac Amarú revolt in Peru.
1791		Haitian Revolution begins. Wolfgang Amadeus Mozart dies.
1808		Napoleon invades Spain. Beethoven, *Symphony No. 5*
1810–1824	In general, Catholic bishops oppose the independence movements while many lower clergy support them.	Spanish colonies become independent.
1820s–1900s	As Liberal and Conservative governments seek to control the power of patronage, the Catholic Church becomes an instrument of the state.	Latin American republics torn between Liberals and Conservatives.
1822		Brazilian independence declared. Egyptian hieroglyphics deciphered.
1823		Monroe Doctrine promulgated. United Provinces of Central America secede from Mexico. Beethoven, *Missa Solemnis*
1830		Simón Bolívar dies. Emily Dickinson, poet, born.
1846–1848		United States fights war against Mexico.
Mid-1800s	Protestant missions in Latin America begin.	

1858	Latin American Pontifical College opens in Rome.	The Virgin Mary appears at Lourdes. Benito Juárez elected president of Mexico.
1861–1865		US Civil War fought.
1864–1870		War of Triple Alliance fought (Argentina, Brazil, and Uruguay against Paraguay).
1869–1870		First Vatican Council held.
1873-1874		First Spanish Republic
1888		Slavery abolished in Brazil. T. S. Eliot born.
1891		*Rerum Novarum* on capital and labor is issued. Gauguin is in Tahiti.
1898		Spanish-American War fought. C. S. Lewis born.
1899	Latin American Plenary Council meets in Rome.	
1901		Theodore Roosevelt becomes US president. Pentecostal movement begins in Topeka, Kansas.
1906	Azusa Street Pentecostal revivals in Los Angeles include Mexican Americans.	Upton Sinclair, *The Jungle*
1907	First Pentecostal revivals in Latin America—Valparaiso, Chile.	Pope Pius X condemns modernism. Cubist exhibition held in Paris.
1910	Swedish Pentecostals bring Pentecostalism to Brazil.	Mexican Revolution begins. World Missionary Conference held in Edinburgh. Leo Tolstoy dies.
1913	Committee for Cooperation in Latin America (CCLA) formed to unify Protestant mission agencies and churches.	
1914–1917		World War I fought.

1914		Panama Canal opens.
1916-1924		US Marines occupy Dominican Republic.
1916	Protestant missionary agencies meet at the Panama Congress.	
1917		Russian Revolution takes place. First jazz recordings made.
1925	Protestant mission agencies and churches meet at Montevideo Congress.	
1926–1929	Government anticlerical policies in Mexico result in the Cristero Rebellion.	
1929	Protestant denominations meeting at the Havana Congress begin the "latinization" of the churches.	Great Depression begins. Einstein develops unified field theory. First Latin American Communist Conference is held in Buenos Aires.
1936–1939		Spanish Civil War fought.
1939–1945		World War II fought.
1944		Guatemalan Revolution begins. *Casablanca*, film
1946		U.S. Army School of the Americas opens in Panama as a hemisphere-wide military academy to train in counter-insurgency.
1948		World Council of Churches established. Babe Ruth, baseball player, dies. Pan-American Union (founded 1890) changes name to Organization of American States.
1949	**Latin American Evangelical Conference** (CELA) forms in Buenos Aires.	North Atlantic Treaty Organization founded. Evangelist Billy Graham gains nationwide prominence. George Orwell, *1984*

1954		CIA-engineered coup deposes President Jacobo Árbenz and installs military dictatorship in Guatemala.
1955	**Latin American Episcopal Conference** (CELAM) founded in Río de Janeiro. **Church and Society in Latin America** (ISAL) founded.	Bus boycotts take place in Montgomery, Alabama. Juan Perón deposed from presidency of Argentina.
1956	Jim Eliot and four other evangelical missionaries killed in Ecuador.	Jackson Pollack dies.
1959	The Catholic Church initially supports Castro because of his focus on Cuba's poor.	Cuban Revolution overthrows Fulgencio Batista. Frank Lloyd Wright dies.
1961	**Latin American Evangelical Commission for Christian Education** formed in Peru.	Bay of Pigs invasion of Cuba fails.
1962–1965	Vatican II inspires bishops to contextualize theology and practice.	Second Vatican Council held.
1962	The emerging Chicano movement motivates Protestant and Catholic church leaders to develop theologies from a Latino perspective.	César Chávez and Dolores Huerta found the United Farm Workers Association in California. Carlos Fuentes, *Death of Artemio Cruz*
Late 1960s	Christian base communities begin to form throughout Brazil. Catholic Charismatic Renewal movement spreads to Latin America.	
1964	**Provisional Commission for Evangelical Unity in Latin America** (UNELAM) formed in Montevideo, Uruguay.	US government supports military coup d'état in Brazil. Pope Paul VI and Ecumenical Patriarch Athenagoras lift excommunication of 1054. Civil Rights Act of 1964 passed in the United States.
1967	José Joaquín "Yiye" Avila founds Christ is Coming Ministries in Camuy, Puerto Rico.	Langston Hughes, poet, dies. Ernesto "Che" Guevara executed.

1968	Paulo Freire, *Pedagogy of the Oppressed* CELAM II in Medellín, Colombia, declares for the "preferential option for the poor."	Martin Luther King Jr. and Robert F. Kennedy assassinated. Tlatelolco Massacre takes place in Mexico City. Papal encyclical bans artificial contraception. Mexico City hosts the Olympics.
1969	**Latin American Congress on Evangelization** (CLADE) forms in Bogotá.	Astronauts land on moon. Woodstock festival held. Birth of the internet.
1970	**Latin American Theological Fraternity** (FTL) founded.	
1971	Gustavo Gutiérrez, *A Theology of Liberation*	"Jesus movement" attracts young people. First email sent. Pablo Neruda wins Nobel Prize.
1973–1990	Evangelicals support Pinochet while many Catholic and mainline Protestant leaders denounce him and expose human rights abuses.	Augusto Pinochet is dictator in Chile.
1973	**Commission for the Study of the History of the Church in Latin America** (CEHILA) formed.	Yom Kippur War fought.
1975		Operation Condor in South America hunts dissidents.
1976–1983	The church remains silent during the Dirty War.	Argentina's Dirty War occurs.
1978–2005	John Paul II opposes liberation theology and replaces left-leaning bishops with conservatives; his visits throughout the Americas draw thousands.	Papacy of John Paul II.
1979–1990	Several priests, including Ernesto Cardenal, take positions in the Sandinista government.	Sandinista government in Nicaragua.
1979	CELAM meets in Puebla.	Iranian Revolution takes place.
1980–1992	Government militias target Catholic leaders in El Salvador.	Salvadoran civil war fought.

1980	Archbishop Oscar Romero assassinated in El Salvador. Three US nuns and a lay missionary murdered in El Salvador. **Latin American Evangelical Fellowship** (CONELA) founded.	Ronald Reagan elected president of the United States. Mariel boatlift takes place. John Lennon, musician, killed.
1982–1983	Some evangelical churches benefit from the Ríos Montt government in Guatemala.	
1982	**Latin American Council of Churches** (CLAI) established in Peru.	General Efraín Ríos Montt seizes power in Guatemala. Isabel Allende, *The House of Spirits.*
1985-1987		Money from Iran-Contra deals funneled to Nicaraguan Contras.
1985	Women theologians gather in Buenos Aires to discuss liberation theology from the perspective of women.	Mikhail Gorbachev and Ronald Reagan meet for the first time.
1989	Six Jesuits, their housekeeper, and her daughter murdered by US-trained commandos of the armed forces in El Salvador.	US invades Panama. Tiananmen Square demonstrations take place. Berlin Wall falls. World-Wide Web invented. Laura Esquivel, *Like Water for Chocolate*
1990	**Latin American Evangelical Pentecostal Commission** (CEPLA) founded.	School of the Americas Watch founded to demand closure of the military facility.
1991		Soviet Union dissolved. Nirvana, *Smells like Teen Spirit*
1999–2013		Hugo Chávez becomes president of Venezuela.
2001		Western Hemisphere Institute for Security Cooperation opened in Fort Benning, GA as successor to School of the Americas. Terrorists attack the United States.
2005-2013		Papacy of Benedict XVI.

2013	Jorge Mario Bergoglio, archbishop of Buenos Aires, elected as Pope Francis.	Oscar Hijuelos, novelist, dies.

3:3: Regional Organizations

Church and Society in Latin America (Iglesia y Sociedad en América Latina, ISAL): The formation of this ecumenical Protestant organization in 1955 was influenced by missionary and theologian Richard Shaull's engagement with Marxism as well as then-current theories of Latin America's economic dependency on First World powers. Originally focused on teaching the social responsibilities of Christians, by the mid-1960s it had begun to educate the lower classes according to the methods of Paulo Freire for developing critical consciousness. ISAL was viewed with suspicion by more-conservative evangelical churches and with alarm by North American missiologists such as C. Peter Wagner, who feared its similarities to Catholic liberation theology and Marxist critiques of capitalism. As military dictatorships took over much of Central and South America, ISAL went underground in 1975, becoming the Latin American Ecumenical Social Action.

Commission for the Study of the History of the Church in Latin America (Comisión para el Estudio de la Historia de la Iglesia en Latinoamérica, CEHILA): The philosopher and historian Enrique Dussel formed CEHILA in Quito as an ecumenical organization responding to the emerging consciousness of Latin American scholars to the social, political, and economic backgrounds of the region. Recognizing that the task of writing history is never neutral—neither in context nor in values—the commission represents a paradigm shift in the writing of Latin American history, in particular that of the church. It sought to critically reread the historical sources and to do so from the perspective of the poor and marginalized. To that end, its published works, in particular its magnum opus, the multivolume *Historia General de la Iglesia en América Latina* (1981–1995), not only describe the institutional history of the church but also explain its impact on the people, explore the popular religion of the multitudes, and uncover the hidden tales of regular men and women and their struggles for justice in Latin America. In 1975 the commission established a US branch that has released several publications on the history of Hispanic churches.

Latin American Congress on Evangelization (Congreso Latinoamericano de Evangelización, CLADE): This organization was the regional expression of the World Congress of Evangelism sponsored by the Billy Graham Association and held in Berlin in 1966 in order to stimulate evangelistic planning across denominational lines. The first meeting of CLADE was held in Bogotá in 1969. Formed within the context of CELAM's "preferential option for the poor" and with a membership made up primarily of pastors and theologians whose lives and ministries deeply connected with those of the needy, CLADE also sought to address the social and economic ills of the region. Subsequent meetings (Huampaní, Peru, in 1979; Quito, Ecuador, in 1992; Quito, Ecuador, in 2000; and San José, Costa Rica, in 2012) sustained this intersection between evangelism and social justice, in great part due to Protestant theologians sympathetic to liberation theology.

Latin American Council of Churches (Concilio Latinoamericano de Iglesias, CLAI): In 1978 in Oaxtepec, Mexico, the idea of creating an organization to promote Christian unity and cooperation was formed. CLAI emerged in Huampaní, Peru, in 1982. It is a decentralized organization with offices in five subregions to help fulfill one of its most important goals: to accompany local congregations in their daily life and context. It seeks to promote the unity of believers, to encourage and support its members in their evangelistic work, and to promote theological and pastoral reflection and dialogue in the continent. Since the 1980s, in light of the changing state of Latin American nations—namely, the end of several civil wars and return to democracy and stability—CLAI has widened its approach to visibly address issues of social justice such as women, the environment, and the economy and to include the fast-growing Pentecostal churches within its scope. In addition to its 1982 founding meeting, CLAI has come together in Indaiatuba, Brazil (1988), Concepción, Chile (1995), Barranquilla, Colombia (2001), Buenos Aires, Argentina (2007), and Havana, Cuba (2013).

Latin American Evangelical Commission for Christian Education (Comisión Evangélica Latinoamericana de Educación Cristiana, CELADEC): Created in Peru in 1961, CELADEC was dedicated to promoting Christian education and providing Protestant churches in Latin America with educational resources. One of its main publications is the *New Life in Christ Course* (*Curso Nueva Vida en Cristo*), based on the realities of Latin American life. By the 1970s, CELADEC had become the main center of popular Christian education in Latin America. It eventually began to represent a Protestant liberationist standpoint, using its resources to research, publish, educate, and counsel on issues such as human rights, poverty, women, and literacy.

Latin American Episcopal Conference (Consejo Episcopal Latinoamericano, CELAM): This, without doubt, is the most important of the region's international organizations. It was formed in 1955 at Rio de Janeiro to bring together representatives from the bishop's conferences of twenty-two Latin American (and Caribbean) nations. Since the 1960s the conference has set the tone for ministry and theological reflection for the Roman Catholic Church. Its pronouncements have influenced the course of Protestantism and have reverberated across Latin American societies. It has also been the battleground for larger political struggles within the Catholic Church itself. The reforms of the Second Vatican Council, redefining the church as the "people of God" and encouraging bishops to contextualize the gospel and become involved in the struggle of the poor, served as a catalyst to ministerial and theological forces already brewing throughout Latin America.

At CELAM's second meeting, held in Medellín, the bishops addressed the challenges of poverty and violence, declaring that they were not results of a lack of economic development but rather came from government oppression and domination by First World countries. The conference voiced a "preferential option for the poor" based on the witness of the Bible and the recognition that ministry and theology do not begin from a state of neutrality but reflect already present values and commitments. This "option" represented a historic shift from allying with governments to advocating for the poor and addressing their physical and sociopolitical needs as part and parcel of addressing their spiritual ones. As part of its pastoral commitment, the bishops supported the formation of Christian base communities to empower the laity in their understanding of the Bible, spiritual development, and consciousness-raising. While not an example of liberation theology in itself, Medellín provided the foundation for the development of liberation theology in the later

1960s and 1970s. By the time of CELAM's third meeting, held in Puebla, Mexico, in 1979, the Vatican had already taken a disapproving stance toward liberation theology for its confrontational nature vis-à-vis the state and for its reliance on Marxist categories. Led by López Trujillo, the conference had begun a pendulum swing to the right, as had the Latin American church itself in the appointment of conservative bishops under Pope Paul VI, a process that would gain momentum under John Paul II's determined efforts to stamp out the new theology. Prominent liberation theologians were deliberately kept out of the meeting, which was attended by the new pontiff, who, while addressing the scandal of poverty, had nonetheless publically attacked some of the more controversial aspects of liberation theology. López Trujillo sought to undo Medellín, but sympathetic bishops kept the liberationists abreast of developments and documents, and their influence on the final outcome of the meeting was evident. The final document was a compromise hybrid of conservative, moderate, and progressive elements that was interpreted by the champions of each segment as representing their views.

CELAM IV, held in Santo Domingo, marked the quincentenary of the encounter between the Old and New Worlds. The bishops focused on the challenges of the "New Evangelization"—promoting human rights and justice, strengthening the role of the laity, and improving pastoral care as outcomes of Medellín's and Puebla's "option for the poor."

The most recent general conference, this time at Aparecida, Brazil, in 2007, called for a "Great Continental Mission," recognizing that despite Catholicism's near monopoly for five hundred years, many do not participate in the life of the church. Aparecida also voiced an ecumenical imperative in light of a growing secularization and the continuing need to address social, economic, and environmental crises. It continued to hold to the "preferential option" as well as liberation theology's social discernment praxis of "see-judge-act" within the central context of the Lordship of Jesus Christ as Savior of the world. The fact that Argentine archbishop Jorge Bergoglio had a strong hand in the final composition of this document has brought renewed attention to the meeting in light of his election to the pontifical throne.

Latin American Evangelical Conference (Conferencia Evangélica Latinoamericana, CELA): In 1949, eighteen churches came together in Buenos Aires for the first initiative of its kind in Latin America. In great part, this conference was the result of Latin America's exclusion from the Edinburgh Missionary Conference of 1910 under the assumption that the continent was already evangelized. Latin American evangelicals vehemently disagreed; on their agenda were evangelization, the presence of Protestantism in Latin America, and unity between different church bodies. The second conference met at Lima in 1961. It lamented the continuing fragmentation of the evangelical churches and called for them to become more deeply invested in the social problems of the region. Some denounced the congress as communist, resulting in the detention of several of its leaders by the authorities. By this time, Protestantism in Latin America had begun to fragment between those starting to formulate theological and ministerial approaches contextual to Latin America, including ecumenism and social work, and more conservative churches focusing on maintaining a certain type of orthodoxy and dedicated to evangelism. CELA III, held in 1969 in Buenos Aires, included Pentecostals among its members for the first time and also observers from the Roman Catholic Church, who attended as a result of both the social, political and economic changes then taking place in society and the new challenge of dialogue coming out of the

Second Vatican Council. This represented a paradigm shift for the Protestant churches, one that did not please more-conservative churches harboring historic and long-held suspicions of Catholicism. Additionally, some organizations accused the conference of not going far enough in its social commitment and of representing US imperialism. North American commentators rang the alarms of theological liberalism and compromise, but for others it was evident that CELA III marked a stage of maturity within Latin American evangelicalism wherein native denominations stepped forth to create indigenous churches fixed within their own identities and the challenges and needs of their own people, regardless of the priorities and shock of their former US mentors.

Latin American Evangelical Fellowship (Confraternidad Evangélica Latinoamericana, CONELA): Affiliated with the World Evangelical Alliance, CONELA was founded in Panama in 1982 with the support of the Billy Graham Evangelistic Association, the Luis Palau Evangelistic Association, and other conservative Christian organizations. It began as a reaction to Protestant churches considered too liberal because of their ecumenical relationships with the Catholic Church (as in the case of CLAI) or their insistence on addressing social needs and their structural causes, an approach considered too close to Marxist-inspired liberation theology for comfort. Inspired by the Lausanne Committee on World Evangelization, CONELA establishes dialogue, fellowship, and cooperation toward the task of evangelization, particularly among unreached populations. In addition to its founding meeting in 1982, it has met in Maracaibo, Venezuela (1986), Acapulco, Mexico (1990), Miami, Florida (2001), Panama City, Panama (2004) and Bogotá, Colombia (2007). Some have questioned whether CONELA truly represents a Latin American identity: its offices and most of its leaders and broadcasters are headquartered in the United States, its financial support comes from major US evangelical associations, and, beholden to local and regional governments for access to radio, television, and other platforms, they tend to toe the line when it comes to political authority.

Latin American Evangelical Pentecostal Commission (Comisión Evangélica Pentecostal Latinoamericana, CEPLA): The cause of Pentecostal unity has its roots in the cooperation demonstrated by Chilean Pentecostal churches during a series of earthquakes in the 1960s. When the **Latin American Council of Churches** was formed in Mexico, Pentecostal leaders carried forth the conversation, resulting in the founding of CEPLA in Santiago de Chile in 1990. The organization focuses on particular Pentecostal challenges and concerns, evangelism, the study of Latin American Pentecostal history, ministerial training, and unity. Unlike many other conservative groups, CEPLA maintains ties to CLAI and the World Council of Churches, and it engages in dialogue with the Roman Catholic Church. In 2001, CEPLA met in Barquisimeto, Venezuela, and called for the creation of a larger council of Pentecostal churches of Latin America and the Caribbean so that the churches could work together on ecumenical witness, worldwide evangelization, and the particular contributions that Pentecostalism has to make within the Latin American and Caribbean context.

Latin American Theological Fraternity (Fraternidad Teológica Latinoamericana, FTL): Conservative evangelicals who attended the first meeting of the **Latin American Congress on Evangelization** in 1969 became concerned about what they perceived as the heavy influence of liberation theology on the pronouncements and goals of the organization. Individuals across denominational lines came together in Cochabamba, Bolivia, the next year to form the FTL. These were people who neither ignored the deep-pressing social needs of the region in favor of a purer evangelistic message nor wanted to move so far to the left as CLADE. Instead, they sought to reflect theologically and engage the particular Latin American social context from an evangelical biblical hermeneutic. During the 1970s they sponsored meetings touching on a number of themes so as to encourage dialogue on ministry and response to social needs. This organization, made up of individuals, not denominations, represents some of the diversity within socially conscious evangelicalism. Some continue to associate with the Latin American Council of Churches. Others have participated in the Lausanne Conferences while remaining apart from that group's fundamentalist currents. Rooted within the Latin American experience of the people, they encourage the formation of a distinctive evangelical theological expression as a means of transformation and change.

Provisional Commission for Evangelical Unity in Latin America (Comisión Provisoria Unidad Evangélica Latinoamericana,UNELAM): Formed in 1965, this organization, supported by the World Council of Churches, had as its goal the promotion of ecumenical unity in Latin America. It dissolved with the formation of the **Latin American Council of Churches.**

3:4: Maps

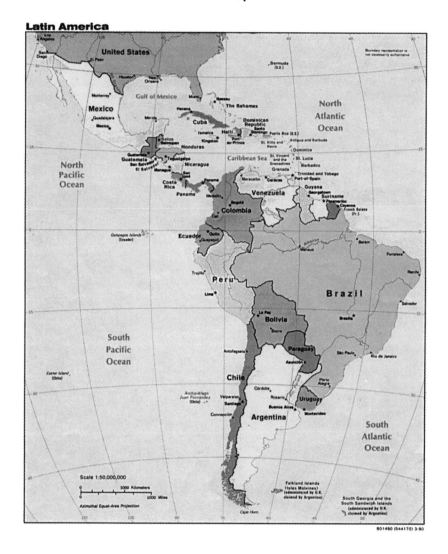

4

Religious Traditions

4:1: Roman Catholicism

Brought by the Spanish and Portuguese to the New World in the sixteenth century, Roman Catholicism has become part of the grain of Latin American identity and culture. Its influence has been present in every facet of life from politics to popular entertainment. About 68 percent of the population professes Roman Catholicism, which is still the region's dominant religion.

4:1:1: Roman Catholic Religious Orders

Roman Catholic religious orders and organizations have been instrumental in the Christianization of Latin America since Europeans first landed on shore. Their history, like all human endeavors, has been mixed: they evangelized, they exploited, they established schools and hospitals and oversaw inquisitions, and they both enslaved and battled slavery. Throughout the continent's history their members have stood behind oppressors and have given voice to the poor, the oppressed, and the dead. Below are some prominent religious orders and movements that have played a significant role or have emerged from Latin American Christianity:

Augustinians (OSA): Formed in 1244, the Order of Saint Augustine was among the earliest religious orders to enter Latin America and is one of the most extensive. From the sixteenth century they labored in Mexico (1533), Peru (1551), Ecuador (1573), Argentina, Bolivia, Chile, Colombia, Panama, and Venezuela (all 1575).

Belemites (Bethlehemites): Dedicated to Our Lady of Bethlehem, this order was founded by Pedro de Betancur in seventeenth-century Guatemala to care for the sick.

Carmelites (OCarm): The medieval Order of the Brothers of Our Lady of Mount Carmel continues their mission throughout Latin America in areas including spiritual development and service.

> **Discalced Carmelites** (OCD): This reformist branch founded and made famous by Teresa of Ávila has among its members Saint Teresa of the Andes from Chile.

Christian Brothers, De La Salle (FSC): This teaching congregation founded in seventeenth-century France by Jean-Baptiste de la Salle has labored throughout the Americas in education. Miguel Febres Cordero of Ecuador, canonized in 1984, was among their members.

Dominicans (OP): The Order of Preachers was prominent in the evangelization of the Americas, dedicated to teaching the indigenous people the Christian faith. Their greatest distinction lies in giving rise to some of the first defenders of the Indians, including Pedro of Córdoba, Antonio de Montesinos, and Bartolomé de Las Casas.

Franciscans (OFM): The friars minor rank among the most prominent in Latin American history. They supported Columbus in his endeavors and were among the first evangelists of the New World. Inspired by the mystical, eschatological writings of medieval writer Joachim of Fiore, they sought to convert natives in mass numbers before the end of the age.

> Franciscan Missionary Sisters of Mary, Help of Sinners Franciscan Sisters of Mary Immaculate Sisters of Saint Francis of the Immaculate Conception (OSF)

Hieronymites (OSH): Dedicated to Saint Jerome and living the Rule of Saint Augustine, members of this enclosed, contemplative order were active as the king's agents for reform in the Caribbean. However, their most famous representative in the Americas has been the polymath and early proponent of women's rights Sor Juana Inés de la Cruz of seventeenth-century Mexico City.

Jesuits (SJ): The Society of Jesus has, in addition to the traditional vows taken by members of religious orders, its distinctive vow of obedience to the pope. Dedicated to mission and education, the Jesuits founded and staffed some of the finest universities of colonial America and established the renowned missions among the Guaraní in Brazil and Paraguay (featured in the 1986 movie *The Mission*). Their power and independence from regal control made them targets for attack, however, and the Jesuits were expelled from Spain, Portugal, and their colonial holdings in 1767. Suppressed in 1773, they were restored in 1814. In modern times, they have been active theologically and pastorally on behalf of the poor and oppressed peoples of the Americas—sometimes to the point of martyrdom, most notably in El Salvador in 1989.

Legion of Christ (LC): Founded in Mexico in 1941 by Marcial Maciel, the Legion of Christ is organization made up of priests and seminarians dedicated to advancing the mission of God in the world. The order has been highly criticized for its alleged practice of "blind allegiance" and for pressuring young people to enter vocations. Allegations of sexual misconduct on the part of Maciel have further marred the congregation's reputation.

Maryknoll (MM): Founded in 1911 and dedicated to overseas mission, Maryknoll consists of a society of apostolic life for men, a religious institute for women, and a lay group. In Latin America, members of the order have worked to alleviate poverty and improve the lives of the poor. Ita Ford and Maura Clarke both worked among refugees in El Salvador until their murder by government troops in 1980.

Mercy of the Americas, Sisters of (RSM): This is an outgrowth of the Sisters of Mercy of the Union, which itself has its roots in the nineteenth-century United States. Founded in 1991, they work across the United States, the Caribbean, and Central America.

Mercedarians (OdeM): Originally organized in thirteenth-century Spain to redeem captives taken in war, the Order of Our Lady of Mercy became a mendicant order, spreading throughout Western Europe and into Latin America to convert the natives. The friars and nuns of the order dedicate themselves today to education and social justice as modern extensions of their original purpose.

Missionaries of Guadalupe (MG): Founded in 1949 and given approval in 1953, this Mexico City–based order has foreign evangelism and the training of indigenous clergy as their goals. Their ministry has spread to the United States, Peru, Brazil, Cuba, Italy, Japan, and Hong Kong.

Missionary Sisters of Mary Immaculate and St. Catherine of Siena: This religious congregation was formed in 1914 by Laura Montoya Upegui, now Colombia's first native-born canonized saint. Originally intended to serve as a missionary order to overcome common prejudices and evangelize among Amerindian communities, the order is now active throughout the Americas, Europe, and Africa.

St. John of God, Brothers Hospitaller of (OH): Founded by the Portuguese adventurer-turned-contemplative John Ciudad, the Brothers Hospitallers were founded in 1572 to serve the sick. From the colonial era they served in Latin America, establishing some of the region's oldest hospitals. Today they are spread throughout Europe, South America, Africa, and the Far East. They have produced doctors, surgeons, and chemists dedicated to helping the disabled and ill.

Salesians (SDB): Named in honor of St. Frances de Sales, this men's and women's order was begun by Don Bosco in 1859. Dedicated to education among the poor, the order is now active worldwide, including in South America. It is the third-largest missionary organization in the world.

Vincentians (CM): Present in Latin America since the nineteenth century, the Society of Saint Vincent de Paul was named after its sixteenth-century founder. This worldwide organization is committed to serving the poor through programs that include food pantries, job training, disaster relief, housing aid, and care for the elderly.

Xavier Missionaries of Yarumal (MXY): In 1927, Miguel Angel Builes founded the Yarumal Missionaries, otherwise known as the Institute for Foreign Missions–Yarumal, in Medellín, Colombia. As Latin America's first missionary society, it sought to evangelize among the native peoples of Colombia. Nowadays its ministers work throughout the Americas, Africa, and Asia.

Other Catholic Organizations and Movements

Catholic Action: Throughout many Roman Catholic countries beginning in the nineteenth century, laypeople began to organize under the direction of local bishops in order to exert a Catholic influence in society. These groups usually formed in reaction to anticlerical governments or in the face of growing secularization. In many countries such as Peru, they were composed of mainly middle-class Catholics. In others such as Chile, they took the form of youth movements. Taking their cues from the social encyclicals of the church promoting the welfare of the poor and the rights of labor, the movement supported candidates and initiatives that would reflect a Catholic social vision. Though not a political party, these lay movements merged in some countries with Christian Democratic parties, especially in the struggle against communist parties in the early to mid-twentieth century.

Christian Base Communities: Also known as Christian ecclesial communities (CEBs), these came to being in the 1960s and early 1970s throughout Latin America and are often associated with liberation theology. They were formed in the aftermath of the Second Vatican Council and CELAM's meeting in Medellín in 1968. Recognizing the scarcity of priests, particularly in rural areas, as well as the imperative to empower the laity after Vatican II, peasants and the poor were often organized under the oversight of a local priest or lay leader. Groups met to study the Bible and were encouraged to discuss it among themselves. This in itself was empowering, allowing belief and reflection to come from the grassroots. The influence of liberation theology also meant that an effort was made to raise consciences—to enable groups to read the Bible and discuss it within the contexts of their own struggles and from there to take action to improve their lives through political or labor initiative. The example of CEBs most familiar to many is that of the poor fishers and artisans of Solentiname in Nicaragua led by Ernesto Cardenal and whose commentary on the Bible was published as *The Gospel According to Solentiname.*

Cursillo Movement: The "short course on Christianity" was founded in Spain in 1944. It is a three-day Roman Catholic workshop for laypeople that focuses on spiritual development and leadership skills within a group setting. Its aim is to empower lay leaders to live Christian lives and influence society around them through the power of their testimony. Colombia became the first Latin American country to host the retreats. Since then it has spread throughout Latin America and has been adapted for other languages throughout the world. In many real ways the Cursillo movement anticipates the Christian base communities associated with liberation theology that developed in the late 1960s and 1970s. Both focus on lay development within group settings in order to address the challenges of daily life.

Delegates of the Word: Like Christian base communities, the Delegates of the Word movement was a response to the both the imperatives of the Second Vatican Council and to the pastoral needs of Latin America, particularly in rural, isolated areas underserved by trained clergy. Delegates of the Word were trained laypeople who served as catechists in their communities or who traveled from village to village to teach, pray, and counsel others. During the civil wars in Guatemala and El Salvador, delegates were among those targeted by right-wing militias, suspected of spreading sedition and communism.

Opus Dei: Founded in Spain in 1928 and approved by the Vatican in 1950, this movement is dedicated to the notion of calling people to holiness within their everyday lives. Most of its members have ordinary family lives with secular careers. A smaller number are celibate and live within the movement's centers. Under the supervision of a bishop and a priest, it organizes workshops in Catholic spirituality as applied to regular life. In essence, the movement follows the tradition of tertiary orders popular in the Middle Ages whereby laity followed the monastic life without necessarily taking any vows. The spirituality of Opus Dei can be described as both applying contemplative practices to secular life and turning everyday work into a form of prayer. In recent decades the movement has gained a negative reputation for secrecy, the mortification of the body in practices such as flagellation, and extreme conservatism (the outlandish novels of Dan Brown have not helped its public perception either). After some reticence by previous pontiffs, Pope John Paul II heavily favored it, canonizing its founder in 2002. Aside from its ministry throughout Latin America, Opus Dei has taken on more powerful roles such as running universities, publishing houses, and training centers in various countries. John Paul II was known to replace outgoing bishops favorable to liberation theology in Latin America with Opus Dei prelates who would not stir up trouble for either Rome or the secular governments.

4:1:2: Major Religious Festivals

Historically Roman Catholic, to a great extent, the nations of Latin America continue to follow the Catholic calendar of celebrations and observances. Countries vary in their official recognition of the holy days; businesses and government offices may close on the feast day of the Immaculate Conception (December 8) in some nations but not in others, for example. Below is an overall listing of religious festivals in Latin America with a short description of how they are generally observed. Distinctive national customs are described in that particular country's chapter in the expanded *Histories of the Latin American Church: A Handbook*, also published by Fortress Press.

January 6	**Epiphany (Three Kings' Day):** The Feast of the Epiphany is observed throughout Latin America in similar ways. The night before, children typically leave their shoes or boxes out with grass or straw for the camels of the Three Magi who visit during the night to leave gifts. The following day is one of relaxation and celebration with friends and family. Though the holiday has been increasingly edged out by the US focus on Santa Claus and on Christmas as the gift-giving day, the retention and rediscovery of Epiphany traditions is a way for many to keep the religious meaning of the Christmas season and to resist North American capitalism and marketing.
March–April	**Holy Week:** Throughout Latin America, this weeklong observance of Christ's path to the cross and the resurrection is typified by dramatic reenactments of the events connected to the Passion from the entry into Jerusalem to the crucifixion and beyond. In traditions brought over by Spaniards and Portuguese during the colonial era, various confraternities, whose membership is passed from generation to generation, take charge of certain aspects of these observances, including the images that are processed down traditional routes throughout the week. These public rituals help form community identities: as the people of God or the church gathered in common devotion and as smaller communities made up of those who oversee and enact particular traditions.

May–June	**Corpus Christi:** This summertime celebration of the miracle of the Eucharist helped define the contours of Latin American society in the colonial era when processions of the consecrated host were displays and confirmations of social hierarchies. Today, it is marked throughout the region by a mass and, in some places, public processions of the Eucharist. Various areas stage elaborate celebrations composed of century-old traditions accompanied by dancing and music.
November 1–2	**All Saints' Day / All Souls' Day:** All Saints' Day or All Souls' Day (some countries celebrate one day rather than the other), often referred to as the Day of the Dead, is especially popular in areas that retain many of their indigenous traditions, some of which have been mixed with Catholic remembrances of the departed. Typically, families visit the graves of their loved ones to wash and adorn them with flowers or fruit. Native American beliefs about the immediacy of the dead during this time of year has resulted, in some places, of the tradition of sharing a meal with the departed or leaving offerings of their favorite food or drink at home altars dedicated to their memory.
December 8	**Immaculate Conception:** The observance of the birth of the Virgin Mary without the stain of original sin is an important festival in this Mary-haunted region, even if it is not celebrated with the visibility and raucousness of Christmas or Holy Week (save in Nicaragua). Special masses are sung and novenas held at churches and private homes in her honor, ticking off the days until Christmas.
December 25	**Christmas:** Though the influence of US market and popular culture has become visible throughout Latin America in the last several decades, with Christmas trees and Santa Claus popping up in what is essentially a summer holiday for many, traditional nativity displays continue to be the centerpiece of public and private observance. The focus of the holiday itself is Christmas Eve, when families gather to celebrate traditional meals before heading out to Midnight Mass. Fireworks, sometimes in elaborate displays, are a normal part of the festivities. Christmas Day itself is often spent quietly with family or visiting friends.

4:1:3: The Virgin Mary

Devotion to Mary was brought to the Americas by Spanish and Portuguese conquerors for whom she served as both mother and warrior. To the medieval emphasis on her gentleness, accessibility, and motherly intercession before Jesus were added battle-ready qualities that came from centuries of struggle against Iberian Islam.

In the New World, the Virgin became a ubiquitous figure as both patroness of the conquest and mother to a conquered people. Here, she became identified and intermingled with Amerindian beliefs such as the Andean Pachamama. The introduction of African slavery added another element into the mix, creating new incarnations as Yoruba deities such as Oshún, Yemayá, or Obàtálá were venerated under the Virgin of Charity of Cobre, Our Lady of Regla, or Our Lady of Mercies. Throughout Latin America, she also carries nationalist sentiment as particular devotions like Our Lady of Luján, the Virgin of Guadalupe, or the Virgin of the Thirty-Three (to name a few) are identified with critical moments in the histories of nations or the experiences of her people. The following are some of her more popular incarnations. Devotions that serve as the patron saint for a country are indicated with the letter *p* noted parenthetically.

> **Argentina:** Our Lady of Luján (p), Immaculate Conception, Our Lady of Itati, Virgin of Cuyo, Black Virgin of Oropa
>
> **Bolivia:** Our Lady of Copacabana (p), Virgin of Candlemas, Virgin of Urcupiña, Our Lady of Mercies, Our Lady of Mount Carmel, Our Lady of Capucdana
>
> **Brazil:** Our Lady Aparecida (p), Immaculate Conception, Our Lady of Nazareth
>
> **Chile:** Our Lady of Mount Carmel of Chile (p), Our Lady of the Forty Hours, The Immaculate Conception, Virgin of Andacollo
>
> **Colombia:** Our Lady of Chiquinquirá (p), Our Lady of the Most Holy Rosary, Virgin of Candlemas
>
> **Costa Rica:** Virgin of Los Ángeles (p), Immaculate Conception
>
> **Cuba:** Virgin of Charity of Cobre (p), Our Lady of Regla, Our Lady of Mercies
>
> **Dominican Republic:** Our Lady of Altagracia (p), Our Lady of Mercies
>
> **Ecuador:** Our Lady of Quinche (co-p), Virgin of Mercies, Our Lady of Good Success, Virgin of Guayco, Virgin of Quito
>
> **El Salvador:** Our Lady of Peace (co-p), Virgin of Guadalupe

Guatemala: Our Lady of the Rosary (p), Virgin of Guadalupe, Virgin of the Assumption

Honduras: Virgin of Suyapa (p)

Mexico: Our Lady of Guadalupe (p), Our Lady of Remedies, Our Lady of San Juan de los Lagos, Virgin of Juquila, Virgin of Zapopan

Nicaragua: Immaculate Conception, Our Lady of Cuapa, Our Lady of the Throne

Panama: Santa María de La Antigua (p), Immaculate Conception, Immaculate Heart of Mary

Paraguay: Virgin of Caacupé (p), Our Lady of the Assumption, Our Lady of Luján

Peru: Our Lady of Mercy (p), Our Lady of Guadalupe

Puerto Rico: Our Lady of Divine Providence (p), Our Lady of Guadalupe, Virgin of the Well

Uruguay: Virgin of the Thirty-Three (p), Our Lady of Luján

Venezuela: Our Lady of Coromoto (p), Virgin of Chiquinquirá, La Divina Pastora, Virgin of the Valley

4:2: Protestantism

Protestant denominations came to Latin America beginning in the nineteenth century when the former Iberian colonies became independent nations. This period, when the new countries sought to expand trade and international relations, coincided with the evangelical zeal resulting from evangelical revivals as well as the expansionist visions of the United States in that period. The small success of historic Protestant missions would be overtaken in the next century by the blazing efforts of Pentecostal evangelists and grassroots movements.

4:2:1: Denominational Missions

Some of the major Protestant denominations with a missionary presence in Latin America include the following:

Antiochian Orthodox Christian Archdiocese
Assemblies of God
Church of the Nazarene
Episcopal Church
Evangelical Covenant Church
Evangelical Free Church of America
Evangelical Lutheran Church in America
Free Methodist Church in Canada
International Church of the Foursquare Gospel
Lutheran Church–Missouri Synod
Mennonite Brethren
National Baptist Convention
Orthodox Church in America
Pentecostal Assemblies of the World
Presbyterian Church in America
Presbyterian Church (USA)
Southern Baptist Convention
United Church of Canada
United Church of Christ
United Methodist Church

4:2:2: Protestant Mission Agencies

In addition to the mission agencies run and operated through the various Protestant denominations (Southern Baptist, Evangelical Lutheran Church in America, United Methodist Church, and so forth), some independent organizations have established a presence in Latin America throughout the last century:

Action International Ministries (AIM): Founded in 1974, it works in eighteen countries including Colombia, Cuba, Ecuador, Honduras, and Mexico among underprivileged and homeless children, prisoners, and impoverished communities.

Association of Baptists World Evangelism (ABWE): An unaffiliated, independent Baptist agency, the Association of Baptists World Evangelism is dedicated to training pastors and supporting churches through long- and short-term mission trips in ten Latin American countries and elsewhere worldwide.

Buckner International: This humanitarian mission agency works among orphans, at-risk children, and families worldwide, including in Guatemala and along the US-Mexico border.

Campus Crusade for Christ International (CCCI): The well-known college campus ministry dedicated to evangelism and humanitarian aid maintains an active presence in virtually every Latin American country.

Central American Ministries (CAM): CAM was instrumental in establishing evangelical churches in many parts of Latin America in the early twentieth century. Today they serve among the most disadvantaged people through housing, education, and other human services in order to foster economic independence. Also known as Camino Global, they have expanded their outreach throughout the global Spanish-speaking diaspora.

e3 Partners: A ministry that focuses on three essential Es of missions—equipping, evangelizing, and establishing churches—they work worldwide, including in nine Latin American countries, organizing prayer groups and mission teams and connecting churches with key national pastors and church leaders. They organize mission trips, some of which are geared toward youth and medical teams.

Fellowship of Associates of Medical Evangelism (FAME): Working with other missions organizations, FAME evangelizes by meeting real physical needs in providing medical facilities, medicines and supplies, and hands-on care through short-term mission teams in a number of countries including Honduras and Brazil.

Food for the Hungry International (FH): The stated mission of FH, founded in 1971, is "to walk with churches, leaders and families in overcoming all forms of human poverty by living in healthy relationship with God and His creation." They work with members to seek an end to world hunger and have assisted with disaster relief efforts, including the response to the 1976 Guatemala earthquake.

Habitat for Humanity International Global Village: The internationally renowned, ecumenical Christian nonprofit organization is dedicated to eliminating substandard housing and homelessness worldwide and to making adequate, affordable shelter a matter of conscience and action. Their ministry was founded on the conviction that every man, woman, and child should have a simple, decent place to live in dignity and safety. They have taken hammer to nail throughout most of Latin America.

Jesus Film Project: Evangelistic in focus, this agency, an outreach of Campus Crusade for Christ, partners with national ministries by taking short-term missions trips to over thirty different countries to give out the *Jesus* film in local languages.

Latin America Mission (LAM): Founded by Harry and Susan Strachan in 1921, LAM is an interdenominational mission agency that seeks to connect missionaries with various needs in the Latin American church, such as social work, theological education, Christian camping, and beyond.

Medical Ministry International: This Christian organization is committed to meeting the need for medical care among the world's poor through patient care and health education. Toward this end, they mobilize volunteers for short-term medical projects and establish as well as equip permanent medical centers. In Latin America they currently have projects in Colombia, the Dominican Republic, Ecuador, Mexico, Nicaragua, and Peru.

New Tribes Mission (NTM): Begun in 1942, this conservative evangelical agency helps local churches train, coordinate, and send missionaries to the over two thousand unreached peoples of the world in Latin America, Africa, and the Asia–Pacific regions.

OM (Operation Mobilization): Since 1957, this evangelical organization has worked throughout the world, including most of Latin America, to help plant and strengthen churches and minister to people through evangelization, emergency relief and development, justice issues, and mentoring.

SIM (Serving in Mission): Formerly Sudan Interior Mission, the organization was founded in 1893; their outreach, now worldwide, seeks to evangelize and minister to human need.

South American Missionary Society International (SAMS): Begun in 1923 and active in Argentina, Chile, and Uruguay, SAMS focuses on evangelism, church camps, and Bible institutes to strengthen local churches.

World Vision: World Vision is a humanitarian organization dedicated to working with children, families, and their communities in nearly one hundred countries.

Wycliffe Bible Translators (WBT): In 1942 William Cameron Townsend founded the Summer Institute of Linguistics and Wycliffe Bible Translators. The former was established to study and preserve the world's indigenous languages. Wycliffe was formed to see the Bible accessible to all people in the language they understand best.

To make this vision a reality, the organization also focuses on literacy development, community development, and church partnerships.

Youth with A Mission (YWAM): Since 1960, YWAM has been an international and interdenominational movement dedicated to evangelism, training, and social ministries such as relief and development. It operates in over one thousand locations in over 149 countries, including a dozen Latin American nations.

4:3: Afro-Latin Traditions

Enslaved Africans arrived in the New World from Spain on the earliest voyages of exploration and conquest. As the Indian population became decimated due to war, violence, and illness, colonists began to request the importation of slaves directly from Africa to work the mines and sugar plantations, particularly in the Caribbean and Portuguese-held Brazil. The first such slaves arrived in Hispaniola in 1502. Spain continued to use British and Dutch slave merchants while Portugal used her own holdings in West Africa. The Catholic Church supported and contributed to this enterprise; missions, churches, schools, and hospitals were built through slave labor. While many church leaders continued to fight the exploitation of the Indians, African slavery was an accepted part of life dating back centuries along the Mediterranean and the church used enforced labor to build and maintain houses of worship and convents, for trade, and in other enterprises. With extremely rare exceptions, churchmen did not address the fundamental issue of slavery (Bartolomé de Las Casas had originally proposed the importation of Africans to replace the natives, but upon seeing the institution in action he recanted his views). Even the evangelization of black people was a low priority. In many cases, Africans were baptized on arriving in the Americas or even, in the case of Portuguese slave merchants, sprinkled with consecrated water as they were boarded onto the slave ships. Their catechetical instruction was limited. They were given rudimentary religious instruction through an interpreter while waiting to be sold at market. Jesuit Peter Claver's lifelong dedication to the spiritual needs of Africans is the exception that proves the rule. The high mortality rate of slaves in Brazil and the Caribbean meant a faster turnover with a constant influx of new slaves arriving, which became a further barrier to the Christianization of these unfortunates. Thus, for example, the worship of *orishas*, minor deities that rule over nature and human endeavor, and the rituals attached to them (altars, ecstatic dancing, possession, and so on) persisted in ways that were unseen, say, in the United States. Quickly discovering that the open practice of African religion could result in rather negative and potentially life-ending consequences in Iberian colonial life, slaves would rename their gods with the names of Catholic saints with whom they shared certain characteristics, allowing old traditions to survive in the New World. For many adherents, there is no discrepancy between belonging to Santería or Candomble and being Roman Catholic. The appropriation of Catholic symbolism to ensure the survival of African traditions served as a means of resistance to colonial powers and testifies to the resiliency of their adherents.

Afro-Caribbean religions, nonetheless, led a practically underground existence until recently. Governments saw them as embarrassing vestiges of the colonial age as they sought to bring their countries into the modern world. The Catholic Church perceived them as superstitious; their reaction ranged from disregard to persecution. The low number of clergy available to catechize anyone, especially in nonurban areas, prevented them from addressing the traditions. With few exceptions, evangelicals and Pentecostals have tended to see Afro-Latin religions through the lens of their own worldview and have often considered them of demonic origin: to be mocked, publically marginalized, and converted from. As Afro-Latin people have sought greater recognition of their place in history and society in recent decades, these traditions have become more visible and, in some locales, organized. Correspondingly, governments have begun to see the practices of the African diaspora as important parts of a country's heritage and to appreciate these religions as potential tourist attractions.

The public visibility of Afro-Caribbean traditions has also meant that these faiths have not remained confined to people of African descent. Individuals of all social classes and racial backgrounds have become adherents. Through the Puerto Rican, Cuban, and Dominican diasporas in the United States, Afro-Caribbean religions have broken their geographical boundaries as well. Today, *botánicas* supplying statues, ointments, and herbs are visible in most Hispanic neighborhoods.

4:3:1: Santería (Regla de Ocha)

The most dominant of the Afro-Cuban religions, Santería, also known as the *regla de ocha* and the *regla de Lucumi*, combines West African Yoruba traditions with Spanish Catholicism. A common variation of Yoruba cosmology posits a distant Creator God, Olodumaré, and a number of created, intermediate beings, *orishas*, who have the power to work on Olodumaré's behalf in the spiritual and natural world (the *orishas* are sometimes considered to be divinized ancestors). *Ashe* is the cosmic energy that connects and animates all things. The *orishas* are the objects of worship and ritual who provide practitioners with powerful *ashe* in return for devotion. Santería ceremonies are mediated by male or female priests known as *olorichás*. The various levels of priests oversee prayers, animal sacrifices, initiations, and ecstatic dances wherein the *orishas* take possession of individuals. Ceremonies typically take place in a *casa de santos* (house of saints), usually the home of the priest, where shrines are erected to the *orishas* in the form of their attributes or Catholic identities. Since Yoruba practices are not exclusionist, adherents are often baptized members and attendees of the Catholic Church. Both as a means of survival and connection to the dominant faith, Santería has since the colonial period identified the *orishas* with Roman Catholic saints that share particular attributes.

Orisha	Sphere	Attributes	Favored by	Catholic Saint
Elegguá	roads, doorways	red and black	for protection, clearing obstacles, soldiers	Saint Anthony
Oshún	sexuality, good judgment, finances	yellow	the lovelorn, businesspeople	Virgin of Charity of Cobre
Ogún	iron and steel	black and green metal tools	doctors, police, farmers, mechanics	Saint Peter
Yemeyá	motherhood, childbirth, children, oceans	blue and white	mothers, sailors	Our Lady of Regla
Shangó	thunder, lightning, fire, masculinity, power, sexuality	red, purple, white	revenge and justice-seekers, protection in storms	Saint Barbara
Orunmila	Knowledge, science, wisdom	yellow and green		Saint Francis of Assisi
Osain	Healing, herbal knowledge	green, gourd	Laborers, home-owners, carpenters, healers	Saint Joseph
Babaluye-Aye	Body, wealth, physical possessions, disease	purple, white, blue broom	AIDS patients, victims of severe illness	Lazarus (from the biblical parable)

4:3:2: Palo Monte (Regla de Palo)

This Afro-Cuban religion originates in the Kongo traditions of the Bakongo people. Palo Monte also takes elements from Catholicism, Santería, and other African-derived religions. Unlike Santería, which emphasizes a relationship with a pantheon of *orishas*, Palo stresses healing and control of the spirits of the dead through charms, spells, and rituals that temporarily inhabit a *nganga*, an iron pot or cauldron and its contents. *Paleros* use elements such as bone, graveyard dirt, spices, plants, and the branches of trees specific to the spirit to create the *nganga*. The spirit is contacted through trances, divination, and ritual. Once captured, it is under the control of the owner. Cauldrons used for good purposes are referred to as "Christian" while those intended for evil are termed "Jewish." The spirits invoked may carry the names of Catholic saints or Santería *orishas*. Practitioners may also adopt the traits of other religions or adhere to more than one, practicing Palo but also Santería, for example.

4:3:3: Spiritism

While spiritism does not have an African or even Latin American pedigree, this system of belief, popularized in the 1800s by the experiences of the Fox sisters in New York and the French educator Allan Kardec, resonated with Caribbean and African worldviews to create a distinctive form of *espiritismo* that has, through Cuban and Puerto Rican communities, also spread to the United States, Mexico, Venezuela, and other parts of South America. Kardec described the spiritualist movement as a moral philosophy, bridging the supernatural with the scientific revolution. At the root of spiritism, of course, is the belief in the immortality of the soul and the afterlife, along with the belief that people in this life can communicate with the spirit world by means of mediums. In the Caribbean, spiritism appealed to the middle and upper classes seeking an alternative to the rigid Catholic orthodoxy they associated with Spanish colonialism. Its beliefs in the ability of the soul to evolve past this life and bring enlightenment to the living allowed the Cuban and Puerto Rican elite to incorporate science and Enlightenment reason. Spiritism was also absorbed by other social classes, abetted by and syncretized with existent African notions of the immediacy of the spirit world. Thus different forms of spiritism emerged in the Caribbean in the late nineteenth and early twentieth centuries. Participants in Table Spiritism held séances in the presence of a medium and used hymns, music, and invocations to call upon the spirits. Practitioners of Rope Spiritism, or *espiritismo de cordón*, formed a circle and through chants, rhythmic stomping, and walking counterclockwise sought to collectively enter a trance in order to seek healing or information from the other world. Crossed Spiritism includes the use of the cauldron of Palo Monte, and in Puerto Rico a syncretic form of spiritism, sometimes called *Santerismo*, incorporates the *orishas* of Santería, introduced by Cuban immigrants, into the hierarchy of spirits leading to God. The spread of spiritism throughout the Caribbean world, along with popular African beliefs in contact with the spiritual world through ecstasy and trance, may partially explain the rapid rise of Pentecostalism in Cuba, Puerto Rico, the Dominican Republic, and Brazil in the last hundred years.

4:3:4: Candomblé

A syncretic Afro-Brazilian tradition that incorporates the beliefs of the Yoruba, Bantu, and Fon peoples who were enslaved and brought to the Portuguese colony, Candomblé mixes the Yoruba *orishas* (*orixás* in Portuguese) with the *voduns* and *nkisis* spirits of the Fon and Bantu as intermediaries under the Creator God, Oludumaré. The religion also posits that every individual has a personal *orixa* who guides the person's destiny and serves as protector. There is no system of prescribed morality; rather, the goal is to live according to one's destiny. The spirits serve to guide one in what is moral. Those who practice evil, in turn, will eventually reap what they sow. As in Santería, ceremonies are conducted by priests in a special house or sacred space adorned with the colors and offerings preferred by the *orixa* to be honored. Choreographed dances and festive music ensure that worshippers are possessed by the *orixás*, who can bring healing or guidance to participants. Even though the first Candomblé temple was erected at the beginning of the nineteenth century, the tradition dates to earlier in the colonial period. Despite the fact that Candomblé's music has influenced the development of Brazilian music in general, it was subject to oppression and persecution until the 1970s. Since then, Afro-Brazilians have been more adamant about their place within Brazilian society and more open about their religious practices. This has resulted in a sense of pride and revival among Candomblé's adherents. Some have traveled to Africa to learn more about the roots of their faith, and others have sought to shear Candomblé's *orixás* of their identification with Roman Catholic saints.

4:3:5: Umbanda

Formed in the early twentieth century, this Brazilian tradition combines African, Catholic, and spiritist ideas. It holds to a supreme Creator God, Olorum (sometimes called Obàtálá or Zambi), under whom *orixás* exist to guide, protect, and heal people through mediums. The *orixás* are identical to those in Candomblé and Santería and are often revered under their Catholic aliases; other times they are described as the forces of nature or the spirits of the dead. Along with spiritism it holds to a belief in the possibility of spirits to learn, evolve, and reincarnate into higher levels. Umbanda rituals differ according to their adoption of other African traditions. Those schools closer to Yoruba or Candomblé will use music, ecstasy, and sometimes animal sacrifice to communicate with the spirit world. Others, while adopting the *orixás*, reject the use of magic, costumes, and other accoutrements in favor of works of charity. Due to opposition by the Catholic Church and, more recently, Pentecostals, the practice of Umbanda has often been clandestine. However, when in 2008 a group of young evangelical men entered an Umbanda *terreiro* shortly before services, disrupting the meeting and knocking over statues of African deities, the police intervened and not only arrested the vandals but also their pastor under the charge of inciting religious intolerance. This historic first resulted in the government's tracking of crimes based on religious identity and also emboldened the Umbanda community to be more open and willing to report cases of religious intolerance to the authorities.

4:4: Folk Religion

Folk religion consists of regional or ethnic religious expressions and beliefs that run alongside, and in some cases fall outside, official beliefs and practices. They are often syncretic in nature, combining elements from traditional religions with those of the dominant or institutional faith. In the past, observers tended to label these devotions, beliefs, and rituals as "superstitions," but that word places a value judgment on others' religious practices and does not recognize that syncretism exists, to some degree or another, in all official and unofficial religious traditions. Early Christianity, a Jewish sect, was eventually expressed in the language and categories of Greek philosophy. Medievals, as they converted to the Christian faith, took accoutrements of their culture, including religious symbols and rituals, and redefined them within a Christian worldview or simply practiced them alongside Christianity. Christmas trees and the Easter bunny, while shorn of their religious meaning today, nonetheless were borrowings and redefinitions taken from Roman and Germanic traditional religions. The talismanic use of the Bible or the Eucharist among some is another example of a popular belief that runs outside defined orthodoxy (while not being necessarily unorthodox) and that goes largely unquestioned or unchallenged by religious institutions. In Latin America, Europeans, Africans, and Amerindians generally comingled easily (despite the early efforts of some religious orders to segregate natives from the "bad" examples of the Spanish), which resulted in amazing and beautiful racial and ethnic combinations (as seen in colonial *castas* paintings). This multicultural, multidirectional give-and-take also resulted in a plethora of religious expressions outside standard ones, such as attendance at Mass or patronal celebrations.

The reactions of institutional churches have varied throughout history. Sometimes, there has been outright persecution as ecclesiastical leaders feared "idols behind the icons," or the continued worship of indigenous or African gods under the superficial form of Catholic saints. A modern example would be the veneration of Saint Death popular among some Mexicans and US Hispanics. In other cases, churches have seen these traditions as benign cultural expressions that do not defy accepted dogma. The custom of visiting the graves of loved ones for a communal meal with the departed on the Day of the Dead can be considered just such an expression. In yet other instances, institutional bodies bow to popular religion and integrate the "wisdom of the faithful" into official belief and practice, giving them festival days, defining ways of celebration, and so forth. The canonization of Catholic saints often begins with such a process as the church makes universal a local veneration of a popular figure. Marian apparitions, such as Our Lady of Guadalupe, are first venerated among the people and may even be opposed by the official clergy before being granted the church's imprimatur. Religious traditions and denominations that hold to a dichotomous worldview (spirit versus flesh, the church versus the world, holiness versus the secular) tend toward harsher and less ambivalent views on folk practices. The antagonistic tone of many Brazilian Pentecostal churches toward African-derived religions or popular Catholic devotions is a case in point.[1]

One aspect of folk religion in Latin America is the veneration in some communities of unofficial saints, historic or legendary figures whose devotion is unrecognized by the Roman Catholic Church either for lack of historical support or dubious or nonexistent orthodoxy. Devotees identify with these saints whose socioeconomic backgrounds or life events are similar to theirs. Even in cases of ahistorical figures like San La Muerte from Argentina, the saint is considered accessible to individuals in a manner that official ones are not. Below is a list of a few of the more prominent ones with a brief description. For more information, please refer to the Popular

---

1. It might be argued that Pentecostalism in itself is an institutionalized form of folk religion. Belief in the immanence of the supernatural, the acceptance of "Spirit-endowed" miraculous objects such as holy oil, belief in divine healing through the medium of sacred objects or holy individuals, the reliance on charismatic leaders that come from the grassroots, biblical and theological interpretations that arise from spiritual revelations or individual understandings rather than from academia or the magisterium, and the locus of spirituality as the felt experience of the believer are elements that might classify it as such. Certainly, the Catholic worldview inherited from the baroque period, the influence of indigenous and African beliefs, and the acceptance of spiritism in part of the Caribbean world provided Pentecostalism with fertile ground on which to grow. However, this argument goes beyond the scope of this book, and I leave it to better women and men to argue its points and validity.

Devotions section in the referenced country in part 2 of the larger Handbook.

Cristo Aparecido: Colonial devotion to a sculpture of Christ (Mexico)

Difunta Correa: Died searching for her husband in the desert (Argentina)

Escrava Anastacia: Legendary African slave tortured for her beauty (Brazil)

Gauchito Gil: A popular Robin Hood–type figure (Argentina)

Juan Soldado: Convicted murderer; now folk saint (Mexico)

Niño Compradito: Andean devotion to the skeleton of a supposed child martyr (Peru)

Niño Fidencio: Folk healer (Mexico)

Oscar Romero: Many support the martyred archbishop's cause for canonization (El Salvador)

Padre Cicero: Popular nineteenth-century Catholic priest (Brazil)

San La Muerte: The bony representation of Death from whom one demands favors (Argentina)

Santa Muerte: A female skeletal saint of last resort (Mexico)

Sarita Colonia: Dying in poverty, she became patron saint of the marginalized (Peru)

Virgin of the Well: A recent Marian apparition with a controversial following (Puerto Rico)

Appendix One: Denominational and Organizational Weblinks

General

Commission for the Study of the History of the Church in Latin
America: http://www.cehila.org

Latin American Episcopal Conference:
http://www.celam.org/index.php

Latin American Council of Churches: http://www.claiweb.org

Latin American Evangelical Fellowship: http://conela.org

Latin American Theological Fraternity:
http://ftlonline.wordpress.com

Argentina

Argentine Episcopal Conference (Roman Catholic):
http://www.episcopado.org

Argentine Federation of Evangelical Churches: http://faie.org.ar

Christian Alliance of Evangelical Churches in the Argentine
Republic: http://aciera.org

Evangelical Church of Río de la Plata: http://iglesiaevangelica.org

Evangelical Lutheran Church of Argentina: http://www.iela.org.ar

Evangelical Pentecostal Confederation: http://fecep.org.ar

Greek Orthodox Archdiocese of Buenos Aires and South America: http://www.ortodoxia.com

Union of the Assemblies of God: http://www.uad.org.ar

Vision of the Future: http://visiondefuturo.org

Bolivia

Bolivian Assemblies of God: http://asambleadediosboliviana.com/

Catholic Church in Bolivia: http://www.iglesia.org.bo

Ekklesia: http://ruibalministries.wordpress.com

Evangelical Christian Union: http://www.ucebolivia.com

Friends National Evangelical Church:
   http://www.quaker.org/christonet/inela/index.htm

Brazil

Brazilian Catholic Apostolic Church:
   http://www.igrejabrasileira.com.br

Evangelical Church of the Lutheran Confession in Brazil:
   http://www.luteranos.com.br

Evangelical Congregational Church in Brazil:
   http://www.iecb.org.br

God Is Love Pentecostal Church: http://www.ipda.org.br/

Independent Presbyterian Church: http://www.ipib.org

Methodist Church in Brazil: http://www.metodista.org.br

National Conference of Bishops of Brazil (Roman Catholic):
   http://www.cnbb.org.br

Presbyterian Church of Brazil: http://www.ipb.org.br

Reborn in Christ Church: http://www.igospel.org.br

Renewed Presbyterian Church: http://www.iprb.org.br

United Presbyterian Church of Brazil: http://www.ipu.org.br

Universal Church of the Kingdom of God:
  http://www.universal.org

Chile

Anglican Church of Chile: http://www.iach.cl

Antiochian Orthodox Archdiocese of Chile:
  http://www.chileortodoxo.cl/arqui.html

Assemblies of God of Chile: http://www.lasasambleasdedios.cl

Council of Evangelical Fundamentalist Churches of Chile:
  http://www.cief.cl

Episcopal Conference of Chile (Roman Catholic):
  http://www.iglesia.cl

Evangelical Lutheran Church in Chile: http://ielch.cl

Lutheran Church in Chile: http://www.iglesialuterana.cl

Methodist Church of Chile: http://www.metodistachile.cl

Methodist Pentecostal Church of Chile: http://www.impch.org

National Presbyterian Church of Chile:
  http://laredencion.site90.net

Union of Evangelical Baptist Churches of Chile:
  http://www.ubach.cl/index.html

Colombia

Colombian Methodist Church: http://metodista.org.co

Episcopal Conference of Colombia (Roman Catholic):
  http://www.cec.org.co

Evangelical Lutheran Church of Colombia: http://www.ielco.org

International Charismatic Mission: http://www.mci12.com

Ministerial Church of God of Jesus Christ, International:
http://www.idmji.org/index.php/en/

Presbyterian Church of Colombia: http://www.ipcol.org

Costa Rica

Costa Rican Bible Churches Association: http://aibccr.org

Costa Rican Evangelical Alliance:
http://www.alianzaevangelica.org

Costa Rican Evangelical Presbyterian Church:
http://iepcr.org/index/Welcome_English.html

Costa Rican Lutheran Church: http://www.ilco.cr

Episcopal Conference of Costa Rica (Roman Catholic):
http://www.iglesiacr.org

Evangelical Methodist Church of Costa Rica:
http://iglesiametodistacr.org

Full Gospel Church of God, Costa Rica:
http://historiaiglesiadedioscostarica.blogspot.com/2012/11/iglesia-
de-dios-evangelio-completo-en.html

Cuba

Conference of Catholic Bishops of Cuba:
http://www.iglesiacubana.org

Cuban Council of Churches: http://www.consejodeiglesias.co.cu

Episcopal Church of Cuba (Roman Catholic):
http://www.cuba.anglican.org

First Pentecostal Church of Cuba: http://pipdc.net

Interdenominational Fellowship of Evangelical Pastors and Ministers
in Cuba: http://s96891025.onlinehome.us/Cimpec/index.html
International Evangelical Church of the Soldiers of the Cross:
http://www.soldadosdelacruz.org
Methodist Church in Cuba: http://www.imecu.com

Dominican Republic

Baptist Churches of the Dominican Republic: http://ibaredo.org
Dominican Episcopal Conference (Roman Catholic):
http://conferenciadelepiscopadodominicano.com/
Dominican Federation of Evangelical Unity: http://codue.org
Evangelical Council of the Assemblies of God in the Dominican
Republic:
http://concilioadrepublicadominicana.jimdo.com
Evangelical Pentecostal Council Ark of Salvation:
http://www.concilioarcadesalvacion.org
Latin American United Pentecostal Church of the Dominican
Republic:
http://www.ipulrd.com
Social Services of the Dominican Churches: http://ssidonline.org

Ecuador

Anglican Province of Ecuador:
http://provinciaanglicanadeecuador.webs.com
Ecuadorian Baptist Convention: http://bautistasec.com
Ecuadorian Episcopal Conference (Roman Catholic):
http://www.iglesiacatolica.ec/web/
Ecuadorian Evangelical Missionary Association:
http://ameeecuador.tripod.com/index.htm

Ecuadorian Federation of Indigenous Evangelicals:
  http://www.feine.org.ec/pacha
Evangelical Apostolic Church of the Name of Jesus:
  http://ieanjesus.org.ec/
Evangelical Church of the Lutheran Confession of Ecuador:
  http://iecleweb.wix.com/newsite#!
Evangelical Conference of the Assemblies of God of Ecuador:
  http://www.ceade.org
Philadelphia Church in Ecuador: http://iglesiasife.com

El Salvador

Assemblies of God of El Salvador:
  http://asambleasdedioselsalvador.blogspot.com
Baptist Bible Tabernacle "Friends of Israel": http://tabernaculo.net
Church of God of the Universal Prophecy:
  http://profeciauniversal.wordpress.com
Elim Christian Mission: http://www.elim.org.sv
Episcopal Conference of El Salvador (Roman Catholic):
  http://iglesia.org.sv/
Evangelical Church of the Apostles and Prophets of El Salvador:
  http://www.ieapes.org
International Tabernacle of Revival:
  http://www.tabernaculodeavivamiento.org

Guatemala

Assemblies of God in Guatemala:
  http://www.asambleasdedios.org.gt
Augustinian Lutheran Church of Guatemala:
  http://iglesialuteranaagustina.org/

Christian Fraternity of Guatemala: http://frater.org

Conference of Evangelical Churches of Guatemala:
  http://www.nuevociedeg.org

El Shaddai Church: http://elshaddai.net

Elim Christian Mission:
  http://www.elimcentral.org/index.php/inicio

Episcopal Church of Guatemala:
  http://www.iglepiscoguate.com/index.htm

Guatemalan Conference of Bishops (Roman Catholic):
  http://www.gcatholic.org

National Evangelical Primitive Methodist Church:
  http://guatemetodista.org

Prince of Peace Church: http://principedepazcentral.org

Honduras

Christian Lutheran Church of Honduras: http://iclh.wordpress.com

Church of God in Honduras: http://www.iglesiadedioshn.org

Evangelical Confederation of Honduras:
  http://www.confraternidadevangelica.org

Honduran Episcopal Conference (Roman Catholic):
  http://www.iglesiahn.org/

Prince of Peace Evangelical Church of Honduras:
  http://www.iglesiaepp.hn

Mexico

Anglican Church of Mexico: http://mexico-anglican.org

Apostolic Church of the Faith in Christ Jesus: http://www.iafcj.org

Assemblies of God in Mexico: http://www.asambleasdedios.mx

Light of the World: http://lldm.org

Methodist Church of Mexico: http://www.iglesia-metodista.org.mx

Mexican Episcopal Conference (Roman Catholic):
   http://www.cem.org.mx

National Baptist Convention of Mexico: http://www.cnbm.mx

National Presbyterian Church of Mexico:
   http://www.presbiterianos.com.mx

Presbyterian Reformed Church of Mexico:
   http://www.iprmsg.org

Theological Community of Mexico:
   http://www.comunidadteologica.org.mx

Nicaragua

Convention of Evangelical Churches of Nicaragua:
   http://cienic.wordpress.com

Evangelical Full Gospel Association:
   http://www.aecnetsite.org

Evangelical Methodist Church of Nicaragua:
   http://www.iglesiametodistanicaragua.com

National Council of Evangelical Pastors of Nicaragua:
   http://cnpen.net

Nicaraguan Episcopal Conference (Roman Catholic):
   http://www.cen-nicaragua.org

United Evangelical Pentecostal Mission of Nicaragua:
   http://mepun.org.ni

Panama

Assemblies of God of Panama: http://asambleasdediospanama.org

Christian House of Prayer: http://www.cocpanama.com

Evangelical Methodist Church of Panama:
  http://www.iempanama.com
Foursquare Church of Panama: http://www.cuadrangular.org.pa
Panamanian Episcopal Conference (Roman Catholic):
  http://www.iglesia.org.pa/nueva

Paraguay

Association of Evangelical Pastors of Paraguay:
  http://www.apepnacional.org.py
Evangelical Church of Río de la Plata: http://iglesiaevangelica.org
Evangelical Lutheran Church of Paraguay:
  http://www.iglesialuterana.org.py
Paraguayan Episcopal Conference (Roman Catholic):
  http://www.episcopal.org.py
People of God Church:
  http://congregacioncristianapueblodedios.blogspot.com
Presbyterian Church in Paraguay: http://www.ipparaguay.org

Peru

Anglican Church of Peru: http://www.peru.anglican.org
Church of God of Prophecy: http://www.cogopperu.org
Evangelical Association of the Israelite Mission of the New
  Covenant: http://www.aeminpu.com.pe
Methodist Church of Peru: http://www.iglesiametodista.org.pe
Peruvian Episcopal Conference (Roman Catholic):
  http://www.iglesiacatolica.org.pe
Peruvian Evangelical Church:
  http://www.iglesiaevangelicaperuana.org.pe
Peruvian Lutheran Evangelical Church: http://www.ilepperu.org

Union of Evangelical Christian Churches of Peru:
   http://www.geocities.ws/luisenriqueweb/pag_web_unicep/
index.htm

Puerto Rico

Church of God, Inc.: http://www.laiglesiadediosinc.com
Church of God Pentecostal, International Mission: http://idpmipr.org
Convention of Baptist Churches of Puerto Rico:
   http://www.cibspr.org
Defenders of the Faith: http://www.defensoresdelafe.org
Methodist Church of Puerto Rico: http://www.metodistapr.org
Missionary Churches of Christ, Inc.:
   http://www.conciliodecristomisionera.org
Pentecostal Church of Jesus Christ, International Mission:
   http://ipjmird.org
Puerto Rican Episcopal Church: http://www.episcopalpr.org
Puerto Rican Episcopal Conference (Roman Catholic):
   http://arqsj.org/conferencia.html
Samaria Evangelical Church: http://www.samariaiglesia.com
United Evangelical Church in Puerto Rico:
   http://iglesiaevangelicaunida.org

Uruguay

Anglican Church of Uruguay: http://uruguay.anglican.org
Assemblies of God in Uruguay: http://www.lasasambleasdedios.org
Episcopal Conference of Uruguay (Roman Catholic):
   http://iglesiacatolica.org.uy
Methodist Church in Uruguay: http://www.imu.org.uy
United Evangelical Lutheran Church of Argentina and Uruguay:

https://luteranaunida.wordpress.com

United Pentecostal Church of Uruguay: http://ipuruguay.org

Venezuela

Association of Evangelical Churches of the East:
  http://www.asigeo.org

Evangelical Council of Venezuela: http://consejoevangelico.org.ve

Evangelical Lutheran Church in Venezuela:
  http://ielv.ve.tripod.com/index.htm

Evangelical Pentecostal Church of the Cross:
  http://www.iglesiadelacruz.com

General Council of the Assemblies of God of Venezuela:
  http://www.asambleasdedios.org.ve

International Light of the World Evangelical Church:
  http://obraluzdelmundo.org

National Baptist Convention of Venezuela: http://www.cnbv.org.ve

Reformed Catholic Church: http://icarven.blogspot.com

United Pentecostal Church of Venezuela:
  http://www.pentecostalesunidos.com.ve

Venezuelan Episcopal Conference: http://www.cev.org.ve

Venezuelan Organization of Evangelical Christian Churches:
  http://ovice.org/home

Latinos in the United States

Academy of Catholic Hispanic Theologians of the United States:
  www.achtus.us

Assembly of Christian Churches: http://www.aicinternacional.org

Assembly of Pentecostal Churches of Jesus Christ, Inc.:

http://aipj.org/index.php

Fountain of Salvation Christian Churches:
http://www.fuentedesalvacion.com

Hispanic Center for Theological Studies:
http://www.chet.org/english/

Hispanic/Latino Affairs, US Conference of Catholic Bishops:
http://www.usccb.org/issues-and-action/cultural-diversity/
hispanic-latino

Hispanic Theological Initiative: http://www.ptsem.edu/hti

Hispanic United Pentecostal Church: http://www.ipuh.us

Latin American Council of Christian Churches:
http://bethelcladic.com

Latin American Council of the Pentecostal Church of God of New
York: http://www.clany.org

Maranatha World Revival Ministries: http://maranathausa.com

National Hispanic Christian Leadership Conference:
http://www.nhclc.org

Rehoboth Council of Christian Churches, Inc.:
http://rehobothchurchsi.com

Appendix Two: For Further Reading

Below are listed several recommendations for further reading. I have sought to include both introductory and advanced resources covering the geography and diversity of Christianity in Latin America that would be most insightful or appropriate for undergraduates, graduate students, and other readers.

General

Christianity in Latin America, by Hans-Jurgen Prien (Brill, 2013).
> An excellent overview by a noted German Protestant scholar that includes European scholarship previously unknown in English; somewhat pricey, it is best available at university libraries.

Christianity in Latin America: A History, by Ondina E. González and Justo L. González (Cambridge University Press, 2007).
> This introduction focuses on the mutual relationships between Christianity and its surrounding culture and the transformations each have affected on the other

The Church in Latin America 1492–1992, edited by Enrique Dussel (Orbis, 1992).
> Written for the five hundredth anniversary of the European

encounter, the chronological surveys and topical sections provide a liberationist perspective to the subject.

New Worlds: A Religious History of Latin America, by John Lynch (Yale University Press, 2012).

This eminently readable introduction covers not only Christianity but also indigenous, Afro-Latin, and other minority religions.

Religion in Latin America: A Documentary History, edited by Lee M. Penyak and Walter J. Petry (Orbis, 2006).

This collection of primary readings begins with native myths and continues to the modern era. Each entry includes background context and questions to consider; the book is an excellent resource for college or graduate introductions.

South and Meso-American Native Spirituality: From the Cult of the Feathered Serpent to the Theology of Liberation, edited by Gary H. Gossen (Crossroad, 1997).

This work provides a window into the many varieties of piety and spirituality throughout the continent.

Colonial

Bartolomé de Las Casas: A Biography, by Lawrence A. Clayton (Cambridge University Press, 2012).

Clayton, an eminent scholar of Las Casas, successfully interacts with the latest scholarship to present an engaging portrait of the famous Defender of the Indians.

Neither Saints nor Sinners: Writing the Lives of Women in Spanish America, by Kathleen Ann Myers (Oxford University Press, 2003).

The variety and roles of religious women in colonial Latin America are highlighted through their own writings, displaying how even in a repressive environment they could occasionally dictate their own lives.

Religion in the Andes: Vision and Imagination in Early Colonial Peru, by Sabine MacCormack (Princeton University Press, 1993).

This thorough investigation of Andean religion looks at the perspectives of both the Europeans and the Indians as they sought to make sense of this new civilization.

Sor Juana, or the Traps of Faith, by Octavio Paz (Harvard University Press, 1988).

Written by Nobel Prize winner Octavio Paz, this book is the gold standard of Sor Juana biographies and has influenced every modern narrative of her life and times. Occasionally dense, it provides a literary-historical look into the seventeenth-century Mexican nun.

The Very Nature of God: Baroque Catholicism and Religious Reform in Bourbon Mexico City, by Brian Larkin (University of New Mexico Press, 2010).

Larkin makes a case for a theological and ecclesiastical sea change in eighteenth-century Mexico by looking at the sermons, pieties, and testaments contrasting the spiritualities of the baroque period and the Enlightenment.

A Violent Evangelism: The Political and Religious Conquest of the Americas, by Luis N. Rivera (Westminster/John Knox Press, 1992).

This is an indispensable book that explores the theological, philosophical, and juridical justifications for the Spanish wars of conquest and the subsequent enslavement of the Indians.

Early Republics

The Catholic Church in Peru 1821–1985: A Social History, by Jeffrey L. Klaiber, SJ (Catholic University of America Press, 1992).

A readable and insightful introduction into the history and transformation of the Peruvian church, this book focuses on important movements and individuals.

From Fanatics to Folk: Brazilian Millenarianism and Popular Culture, by Patricia R. Pessar (Duke University Press, 2004).

Pessar paints a well-rendered portrait of millenarian movements and their contexts throughout Brazilian history, highlighting their interactions with larger society and their adaptations to survive to the present day.

Piety, Power, and Politics: Religion and Nation Formation in Guatemala, 1821–1871, by Douglass Sullivan-González (University of Pittsburgh Press, 2008).

The relationships between church, state, and society are mapped out in this book, which notes how the intersections between national institutions helped form a Guatemalan self-identity.

Protestantism and Political Conflict in the Nineteenth-Century Hispanic Caribbean, by Luis Martinez-Fernandez (Rutgers University Press, 2002).

This work explores the history of Protestant evangelicalism vis-à-vis the Catholic Church and its role within the liberal enclaves of Puerto Rico, Cuba, and the Dominican Republic.

Religious Culture in Modern Mexico, edited by Martin Austin Nesvig (Rowman and Littlefield, 2007).

A collection of insightful articles illustrating the variety of religious expression in Mexico from independence to the twentieth century on a broad range of topics from charitable institutions to Protestant beginnings to religion in the Mexican Revolution.

Modern Period

The Church, Dictatorships, and Democracy in Latin America, by Jeffrey L. Klaiber, SJ (Orbis, 1999).

An excellent history of the Catholic Church's role to defend human rights in Latin America.

The Emergence of Liberation Theology: Radical Religion and Social Movement Theory, by Christian Smith (University of Chicago Press, 1991).

A readable, informative introduction to the social and theological history of liberation theology.

The Gospel in Solentiname, by Ernesto Cardenal (Orbis, 2010).

The impact of base ecclesial communities is witnessed through these grassroots commentaries on the Bible gathered on the island of Solentiname in Nicaragua.

The Rebirth of Latin American Christianity, by Todd Hartch (Oxford University Press, 2014).

An exploration into the social and religious movements throughout Latin America—from evangelicalism to Charismatic Catholicism to liberation theology—that are revitalizing Christianity.

Resurgent Voices in Latin America: Indigenous Peoples, Political Mobilization, and Religious Change, edited by Edward L. Cleary and Timothy J. Steigena (Rutgers University Press, 2004).

An introduction to religious roots and influences on modern indigenous movements on behalf of human and civil rights.

The Rise of Charismatic Catholicism in Latin America, by Edward L. Cleary (University Press of Florida, 2011).

The history and effects of one of the most important spiritual movements in Catholicism today.

Romero: A Life, by James R. Brockman (Orbis, 1989).

The essential biography of the martyred archbishop traces his journey of conscience and action to become one of the world's preeminent defenders of human rights.

Witness to the Truth: The Complicity of Church and Dictatorship in Argentina, 1976–1983, by Emilio Mignone (Orbis, 1988).

A harrowing indictment of the Argentine church's inaction during that country's Dirty War.

Protestantism

Tongues of Fire: The Explosion of Protestantism in Latin America, by David Martin (Blackwell, 1990).

An exploration into the growth of evangelical Protestantism by a noted sociologist.

Is Latin America Turning Protestant? The Politics of Evangelical Growth, by Martin Stoll (University of California Press, 1990).

The history of the modern evangelical movement in Latin America is detailed here, emphasizing its role in affecting and determining the politics of the region.

Faces of Latin American Protestantism, by José Míguez Bonino (Eerdmans, 1997).

A short introduction to the history and various kinds of Protestantisms from a noted theologian.

Evangelical Christianity and Democracy in Latin America, by Paul Freston (Oxford University Press, 2008).

Case studies of five Latin American countries explore whether conservative evangelicalism's role in politics will result in more authoritarian systems or contribute to growing democracy.

City of God: Christian Citizenship in Postwar Guatemala, by Kevin O'Neill (University of California Press, 2009).

In the wake of Guatemala's long civil war, Pentecostal churches have linked national self-identity with religious belief, behavior, and worldview.

Power, Politics, and Pentecostals In Latin America, edited by Edward L. Cleary and Hannah W. Stewart-Gambino (Westview, 1998).

This important book explores the role of a rapidly growing Pentecostalism in defining family life, civic participation, and workplace behavior throughout the continent.

Afro-Latin and Folk Religion

Afro-Caribbean Religions: An Introduction to Their Historical, Cultural, and Sacred Traditions, by Nathaniel Samuel Murrell (Temple University Press, 2009).

A well-researched and thorough survey detailing the survival and adaptation of African traditions in the Spanish-, French-, and English-speaking Caribbean world.

Creole Religions of the Caribbean: An Introduction from Vodou and Santeria to Obeah and Espiritismo, 2nd ed., by Margarite Fernández Olmos and Lizabeth Paravisini-Gebert (New York University Press, 2011).

This accessible introduction, suitable for college students, provides excellent portraits of the Caribbean's major African-derived religions, including Santería, Candomblé, and Vodou.

Cultures of Devotion: Folk Saints of Spanish America, by Frank Graziano (Oxford University Press, 2006).

Graziano explores the world of those popular saints unrecognized by the Catholic Church and looks into their historical and social roots.

Devoted to Death: Santa Muerte, the Skeleton Saint, by Andrew R. Chestnut (Oxford University Press, 2012).

The book dispels some of the misunderstanding surrounding this headline-grabbing saint—found from drug-trafficker dens to local bodegas—and raises issues concerning religious liberty and the social background of popular devotions.

Governing Spirits: Religion, Miracles, and Spectacles in Cuba and Puerto Rico, 1898–1956, by Reinaldo L. Román (University of North Carolina Press, 2007).

The overlap between politics, citizenship, the subaltern, and "acceptable" religion is detailed in this work recounting the reaction of modern Cuban and Puerto Rican societies to long-repressed religious traditions.

Virgin Mary and the Saints

Colonial Saints: Discovering the Holy in the Americas, edited by Allan Greer and Jodi Bilinkoff (Routledge, 2003).

A collection of essays exploring issues of race, gender, politics, and colonial identity through the veneration of saints in Iberian, French, and British America.

From Viracocha to the Virgin of Copacabana: Representation of the Sacred at Lake Titicaca, by Verónoca Salles-Reese (University of Texas Press, 1997).

An important contribution to the intellectual and religious history of the Lake Titicaca region, exploring how the sacred has been appropriated and adapted through the ages of Inca conquest through Spanish domination.

La Conquistadora: The Virgin Mary at War and Peace in the Old and New Worlds, by Amy G. Remensnyder (Oxford University Press, 2014).

This very recent work focuses on the role of Mary as warrior, the transposition of Mary from Spain to the Americas, and how indigenous cultures used her to create their own self-identities.

Mary, Mother and Warrior: The Virgin in Spain and Latin America, by Linda B. Hall (University of Texas Press, 2004).

A recommended introduction to the veneration of Mary and the divine feminine throughout Spain and Latin America, noting how Mary's image and qualities have been used to both assert and resist domineering powers.

Mexican Phoenix: Our Lady of Guadalupe: Image and Tradition across Five Centuries, by D. A. Brading (Cambridge University Press, 2001).

A highly detailed and well-researched epic of the history of the Mexican Virgin's life in piety, devotion, politics, and identity.

Latinos in the United States

Fronteras: A History of the Latin American Church in the USA since 1513, edited by Moises Sandoval (Mexican American Cultural Center, 1983).

Though the older of Sandoval's works on the subject, this book is also his more detailed, surveying the long presence of Latin American Christianity on US soil.

Galilean Journey: The Mexican-American Promise, revised and expanded edition, by Virgilio P. Elizondo. (Orbis, 2000).

This is one of the first works of Latino theology, analyzing the life of Jesus through the perspective of the Mexican-American experience and describing how that interpretation can contribute to the greater life of the church.

Handbook of Latina/o Theologies, edited by Edwin Aponte and Miguel De La Torre (Chalice, 2006).

More than an introduction, this essential overview presents short chapters on the major traditions (Catholic, evangelical, mainline Protestant), dogmas (sin, Christ, salvation), and areas (women, GLBT) within Latina/o theologies.

Latino Catholicism: Transformation in America's Largest Church, by Timothy Matovina (Princeton University Press, 2011).

An overview of the Latino Catholic experience to the present day, this text focuses not only on institutional history but also social activism, family values, piety, and current social and political concerns.

Mañana: Christian Theology from a Hispanic Perspective, by Justo L. González (Abingdon, 1990).

As one of the first and most accessible expositions of Latino theology from a Protestant point of view, this book introduces many of its central themes including marginality, reading the Bible "in Spanish," and the principal Christian themes of the Trinity, the Incarnation, and so on.

Mexican American Religions: Spirituality, Activism, and Culture, edited by Gastón Espinosa and Mario T. García (Duke University Press, 2008).

This valuable collection of essays represents a multidisciplinary look into the role of religion in Mexican-American culture, art, literature, politics, and activism and represents an important contribution to religious, Mexican-American, and US studies.

Protestantes/Protestants: Hispanic Christianity within Mainline Traditions, edited by David Maldonado (Abingdon, 1999).

In a society where most US Hispanics identify as Roman Catholic, this book seeks to explore the history, theological perspectives, social dynamics, and pastoral realities of the Latino Protestant communities.

Index